TOBAGO *in print*

(vol.1)

A collection of works by Tobago writers

Published by the Tobago Writers Guild

Compiled by Deborah Moore-Miggins

Edited by Brenda Caesar & Thelma Perkins

To order additional copies of this book, contact:
Xlibris
1-888-795-4274
www.Xlibris.com
Orders@Xlibris.com
729024

Table of Contents

Introduction to the
Tobago Writers Guild

The Tobago Writers Guild (TWG) was incorporated on February 12, 2010 as a non-profit organisation with the following aims:

- The promotion of writing - creative, historical or otherwise;
- The promotion and improvement of reading;
- The creation of a community of writers;
- The provision of assistance to schools and community based groups in the areas of writing, reading and dramatic presentations; and
- All activities incidental thereto.

The group was formed out of a Writers workshop that took place in 2008. Present were Marlene NourbeSe Philip, award winning author of *Harriet's Daughter* and *Zong*, Deborah Moore-Miggins, author of *The Caribbean Proverbs that Raised Us*, Umilta Roberts-Henry, writer of eulogies and skits and Laureen Burris-Phillip, winner of the Commonwealth Short Story Competition for the region 1996. All participants felt the need for the creation of a writers' group in Tobago.

Regular monthly meetings were held at Laureen Burris-Phillip's home, aimed at refining our aims and objectives and encouraging actual writing by members. There were "open mic" sessions at every meeting when members presented their workwhich included poetry, short stories, calypsos, monologues, and research done on various topics.

As soon as the incorporation process was complete, the guild was launched at a ceremony in April 2010 at the Itsy Bitsy Theatre where work of a very high calibre was presented. Patrons were invited to the show and treated to refreshments. Since then the TWG has held its Literary Affair every year, the latest being its fifth edition on 30th May 2015. In 2012, another annual function was added in October called the Reading Fest where anyone, audience or TWG member could read a favourite piece from any book, journal or anything they have written. This function has its own "crowd" and is greeted with enthusiasm in the latter half of the year.

There has been collaboration in planning the Tobago Word Festival with the Empowerment Foundation of Tobago and, in the last two years, the group participated in the NGC BocasLit Festival in Tobago.

We have also held a writing competition every year since 2010 for all age groups in the areas of calypso, monologue, short story, poetry and play writing. Though the response to our first attempt was not as enthusiastic as we had anticipated we will not be deterred in our effort to encourage all types of writing in Tobago.

The production of this book, Tobago in Print, was the major project for the 2014-2015 period. We hope readers will enjoy reading it. We have allowed each writer the latitude of using the format, font, style and layout that he or she believed would complement his or her work. We hope that readers find this presentation interesting and take no objection to the lack of uniformity in the arrangement.

The current Executive is now: Laureen Burris Phillip (President), Gregory Diaz (Vice President), Brenda Caesar (Secretary), Milcah Robinson-Reid (Treasurer). Membership of the Guild now stands at about 30 persons.

Acknowledgements

The members of the Tobago Writers Guild wish to thank the following persons for their support and encouragement over the last six years: Ms. NourbeSe Philip, Mr. Edward Hernandez (deceased), Mr. Rawle Gibbons, Professor Selwyn Cudjoe, Mr. Andre Phillips and Mr. George Leacock.

We especially thank our members and other persons who submitted their work for inclusion in the book. Special thanks to our President, Mrs. Laureen Burris Phillip, and Secretary, Mrs Brenda Caesar, as well as Mr. Reginald Phillips, and Mrs. Deborah Moore-Miggins, our immediate past President and Secretary, respectively, for their unfailing commitment to the production of the book.

The Tobago Writers Guild is also grateful to Mr. Michael Simmonds for making the COSTAATT facilities available for our monthly meetings for over four years. We also thank Mr. and Mrs. Richard Alfred who allowed us to use the Itsy Bitsy Theatre for many of our functions.

We are especially indebted to Mrs. Deborah Moore-Miggins for coordinating the book and compiling the works, liaising with the contributors and preparing the initial draft. Our deepest gratitude also goes to Mrs. Brenda Caesar and Mrs. Thelma Perkins for devoting long and intense hours to editing the book. We do acknowledge their outstanding efforts in this regard. Of course, each writer accepts final responsibility for the errors and inaccuracies of content in his or her work.

To all members of the public who have attended our productions and supported us generally, we say thank you and express the hope that you will purchase and enjoy this book.

June 2015
The Executive

Foreword

By Marlene Nourbese Philip

Over two decades ago I observed in a poem of mine that English was a foreign anguish. African Caribbean people, descendants of those early Africans brought forcibly to what was mistakenly called the New World, found themselves thrown together with others from different linguistic groups. Communication, the life- blood of relationship, community and survival, would have been a tremendous challenge if you couldn't make yourself understood, or understand others. In addition, colonial powers both forbade the speaking of African languages and forced enslaved Africans to speak European languages, which were never taught.

In the face of the horrific events and circumstances that constitute slavery, the people of the Caribbean fashioned new languages wrought from their African tongues and bodies, their experiences and whatever colonial European language was imposed on them. In my novel, Harriet's Daughter, one of the young protagonists calls it Tobago talk which she wants to learn from her friend who has just come from Tobago. Other terms for this new language are demotic, patwa (as the Jamaicans have termed it), nation language or simply the vernacular. And then there is Standard English, which is needed to be able to function successfully in a modern, globalised world. I have argued elsewhere that we Caribbean people legitimately occupy the full spectrum of langauge, from the demotic or nation language on the one hand to Standard English on the other, and all the hybrids in between.

Tobago in Print (Vol 1): A Collection of Works by The Tobago Writers, published by the Tobago Writers Guild, illustrates the breadth of English expression that is the linguistic reality and heritage of Tobago. More often than not, the Tobago nation language or demotic is employed within the collection to tell folk tales, more traditional stories and explain folk practices. Writers use it for poetry and prose, exploiting the comedy and picaresque nature of the language. Standard English is employed in poetry, some fiction and more expository writing making this a truly bilingual collection. It demonstrates an ease of articulation across the breadth of English as it is used in Tobago.

The content of **Tobago in Print** is diverse and its subject matter wide and generous. The collection includes pieces on folk practices such as speech bands, the lingering racism around skin colour, love stories in poetry and prose, health issues, steel pan, wedding speeches, and stories about village life, all of which are illustrative of the wide interests of the authors.

Tobago in Print is a testament to the importance of The Tobago Writers Guild and its role in the contemporary literary life of Tobago. The Guild, first conceived of at the Scarborough Fort during the 2006 Tobago Heritage Festival, is actually the most recent example in a literary history that goes back to the 1920's and 30's in Tobago. In her opus, **The**

Changing Society of Tobago (Vols. 1 &11), the eminent academic and scholar Susan Craig-James describes Literary Societies in Tobago as early as 1922 (Mason Hall). Through debates, lectures and articles the members of these societies demonstrated their interest and involvement in current affairs both domestic and global. From the perennial issue of Tobago's neglect by the colonial government and Trinidad, through issues related to infant mortality, agriculture, shipping and communication, to the relative influence of Marcus Garvey and Booker T. Washington, the members of these literary clubs engaged with the world. Women were under-represented in the literary clubs of the time, so it demonstrates progress in gender issues that women comprise a majority of the authors in **Tobago in Print**.

No foreword to a publication of this significance is complete without mention of the poet Eric Roach, who, in his poetry about the island of his birth, Tobago, limned the contours of history, culture, politics, folk tradition and memory. In writing from the place that is Tobago, he elevated the island and its circumstances to epic proportions. Tobago and Tobagonians were worthy of poetry – magnificent poetry. Unlike many of his contemporaries, he chose to remain in Trinidad and Tobago and write from those twin islands. There was a time when Caribbean people were nurtured to believe that completion, psychic, spiritual, cultural and economic, could only come by leaving the Caribbean. In "Letter to Lamming" Roach asks: "Why were we born under the star of rhyme/Among a displaced people lost on islands/Where all time past is knotted in time present?" While there still remain many issues to be resolved in the long, slow process of

Tobago's maturation, the writers in **Tobago in Print** suggest that Tobagonians have moved past being "displaced people lost on islands." Indeed, the strength of the collection lies in that very knottedness of the past in the present through the expression of a living folk tradition, which, in turn, allows individuals to explore the many issues that continue to confront us as members of human family. **Tobago in Print** continues the tradition begun in those early literary clubs; it builds on a belief in the validity of a Tobagonian experience and attempts to answer the question posed by Eric Roach, why we were "born under the star of rhyme.

M. NourbeSe Philip

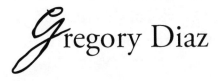Gregory Diaz

GREGORY DIAZ was born and brought up a Trinbago 'Co'ntry boukie'. He says, "A love for all things Trinbagonian burns in me."

"In childhood days, after a dinner of hot coconut bake, home-made chocolate tea and corn porridge cooked on a fire-side in our dirt-floored kitchen, my mother enthralled my three sisters, two brothers and me with local folk tales – some she had heard but most she made up as she went along. Memories of the 'No-head Man' striding through shadows created by a sputtering flambeau are with me even today.

By God's grace, I make every effort to maintain the standard of story-telling given to me by my mother.

Thank you, Mammie.

Thanks also to Ms. Eula Hill, school principal, for reminding me that "there are stories yet to be told."

Legend of the Domesticus Poultricus Animalus -- The "Yard Fowl", or, to cut a long title short, When Cock Had Teeth

Crick! -----------Crack!

In days of long ago -----

-- longer ago than the long ago you thinking is long ago ------

-- longer than that. Much longer than that.

Yes, in days of long, long, long ago, the specie Domesticus Poultricus Animalus, whom we now rudely call 'Yard-Fowl', was a proud, nose-up-in-the-air, high-stepping, higher-faluting breed within the Feathered Community of the Animal Kingdom.

As we now respectfully address men and women as Mr. So and So and Mrs. So and So, the specie Domesticus Poultricus Animalus was addressed as Cock So and So for the males and Hen So and So for the females.

They ate and drank and walked and talked and flew with style and etiquette.

Some, like the Peacock, could boast of the same things; and the Peacock had nicer tail-feathers too.

But one thing raised the specie Domesticus Poultricus Animalus over and above everyone else in the Feathered Community of the Animal Kingdom.

THEY HAD TEETH!

Yes, Cock and Hen had teeth! Real teeth. Sixteen up, sixteen down, thirty two in all. Biters, Chewers, Rippers, Crunchers – they had them all.

And were they proud!

They would step high, point their nose somewhere east of the sun, and grant you a provocative smile.

Not a big, large, wide smile to show-off their teeth. No, they were too proud for that.

Not a little, itsy-bitsy, tiny smile to hide their teeth either. They had something to boast about and they were willing to boast.

The smile was meant to flash all their teeth while reserving a semblance of elegance.

Some folks think it's a tight-lipped sneer.

You'll have to judge for yourself.

But, sad to say, they lost them all; all their flashy shiny teeth.

I'll tell you how it happened and what was the ending of the once-proud Domesticus Poultricus Animalus – the Yard-Fowl.

In days of long ago, well by now you know how much longer ago I'm talking about, in the middle of the Animal Kingdom, on the tip-top of the tallest tree in the Kingdom, sat a powerful jewel called the "Jewel of Contentment".

It wasn't big. It wasn't small. But it was as bright as the lights of seven Suns and eleven Moons. Its light did not burn or hurt the eyes, or keep you awake at night. Instead one just received a soothing caress of joyous light all day and all night that washed you in waves of satisfaction and well-being.

The "Jewel of Contentment" was the pride of all the members of the Animal Kingdom. While shone, everyone lived in harmony and joy reigned supreme. Whatever a body had was sufficient unto that body and bodies gave whole-heartedly unto other bodies whether those other bodies had or not. So everybody's cup ran over.

In other words, everybody was happy.

But you know how some would have all that they could get and still want more? One such was Cock Adodoodledo, youngest of the fifteen children of Cock Whadeycaro and Hen Clu-cluck. Though the "Jewel of Contentment" shone and shone for all it was worth, Cock Adodoodledo just was not satisfied. He had family, friends, food aplenty; house, land, everything a body could possibly need, but he still was not satisfied.

In his heart was a yearning, churning, burning, gotta-have-it-ing hunger that wanted more, **more, more!**

The only thing Cock Adodoodledo did not want was to learn to fly. He saw it as beneath his dignity to engage in such idle behavior when his time could be better spent getting more, **more, more!**

He wouldn't even flap his wings!

His mother Hen Clu-cluck and his brothers and sisters did their best to satisfy his cravings but nothing was ever enough. His father Cock Whadeycaro was just plain upset. He loved his son and it disturbed his spirit to see his son so restless.

One of their neighbors mentioned that maybe Cock Adodoodledo was too far away from the "Jewel of Contentment". Perhaps if he got closer to the tree on which the Jewel was sitting, he would feel the joy of fulfillment.

So the Family decided to hike to the middle of the Animal Kingdom where the tree with the Jewel was growing. But every step that took them closer to the "Jewel of Contentment" made Cock Adodoodledo's cravings worse.

"Oh Mummy, feast your eyes on yonder magnificent house! Could I not have one such?" "Oh Daddy, look at this acreage of land we are traversing, do you not perceive how beautifully it would suit me?" Such were the words of Cock Adodoodledo and his family's spirits were much grieved at his cravings.

After much travel they arrived at the foot of the tree on which the "Jewel of Contentment" sat. Everyone looked at Cock Adodoodledo to see if the Jewel was giving him peace of mind, but the exact opposite was happening.

As Cock Adodoodledo stared up at the "Jewel of Contentment", a wild cry of 'I must have it! Oh, I must have it!' burst from his mouth and with a massive leap he landed on the tree.

The family was shocked. They knew Cock Adodoodledo couldn't fly, wouldn't even flap his wings so how was he scurrying up the tallest tree in the Animal Kingdom so fast?

Jumping from branch to branch, Cock Adodoodledo was soon standing on the tip-top of the tree and in front of him sat the "Jewel of Contentment". An all-consuming yearning, churning, burning, gotta-have-it-ing hunger rose up in Cock Adodoodledo's body, from the tip of his biggest toe to the end of the tiniest feather on his head.

Feeling the need to not only see the Jewel but to taste it too, he opened his mouth as wide as he could and crunched the "Jewel of Contentment" with all the strength of all his teeth, sixteen up, sixteen down, thirty two in all.

And that was the end of Cock Adodooledo's teeth.

With that one big bite, the "Jewel of Contentment" exploded into a million, million pieces and scattered all over the world, and so too did all of Cock Adodoodledo's teeth, all sixteen up and all sixteen down, all thirty two – all gone. Not even the tiniest scrap of a tooth remained in his mouth.

The moment the "Jewel of Contentment" was destroyed, wild behavior entered into the Animal Kingdom. Jealousy, Back-biting, Racism, Hunger and War began everywhere.

Mother Nature, who was resting at the time, woke up in a vexed and revengeful mood. She created a special mighty early-morning wind which snatched Cock Adodoodledo off the tree and flung him tumbling, spinning, twisting and rolling round and round and round the world.

"Find every piece of that Jewel!" roared Mother Nature to Cock Whadeycaro, Hen Clu-cluck and the fourteen brothers and sisters of Cock Adodoodledo. "Until the "Jewel of Contentment" is glued back together, Jealousy, Back-biting, Racism, Hunger and War cannot be stopped. And because it's the teeth of you Yard-Fowl that caused this mess: one - I'm taking away the teeth of all Yard-fowls, all sixteen up and sixteen down, all thirty two of them; two - it's your job to find every piece of that Jewel and make it whole again, and three – Cock Adodoodledo will remain tumbling, spinning, twisting and rolling in the early-morning wind until you do. Maybe if he learns to flap his wings, he won't tumble, spin, twist or roll as much but he's not coming down until the Jewel is remade."

Hen Clu-cluck wept for her son, "Oh, my poor boy! Oh, my poor baby! How can we help him? What are we to do?"

"I'll climb to the highest place I can find when the early-morning wind is passing," said Cock Whadeycaro. "I will call to him and show him how to flap his wings. You take the other children and look for the pieces of the Jewel. Scratch and look. Scratch and look. We don't want to miss a single piece."

So it was said; so it was done.

From then to this day, a father cock climbs to the highest place he can very early in the morning and calls, "Cock-ado-doodle-dooo! Cock-ado-doodle-dooo!" whilst flapping his wings and a mother hen teaches her children to scratch and "Look! Look! Look!" scratch and "Look! Look! Look!"

Jealousy, Back-biting, Racism, Hunger and War are still all over the world because the "Jewel of Contentment" seems hard to find.

It's not.

If you look within yourself you will find a piece of the Jewel and you'll feel the loving warmth of togetherness and harmony it gives. And as you get you must give to others too. The more you give, the more you'll receive.

And please tell the specie Domesticus Poultricus Animalus, the Yard-Fowls, when you've found a piece of the Jewel. They'll be ever so grateful.

The End

Crick! ----------------Crack!

Monkey break he back for a piece of pommerac!

In This Life

Tuparu didn't know what freedom was.

All his life he had been hearing friends and neighbours saying, "We want tuh be free! We go be free! We go dead for freedom!" Hearing such strong desires for 'Freedom!' he also wanted to be free.

But what was this 'Free?'

And how does someone go about getting 'Free?'

Tuparu noticed that no-one who was fighting for freedom had found it. Old, young, rich, poor and everyone in-between, all were striving for a 'Freedom' that seemed reachable but unattainable.

Tuparu lived in Studley Park on the island of Tobago, one-half of the twin-island Republic of Trinidad and Tobago, West Indies. In the year 2014, at fifteen years of age, the main events in Tuparu's life consisted of school at Goodwood High, deep-sea fishing with his father on weekends and public holidays and playing the tenor pan in the Hope Pan Groovers Steel Orchestra.

Tuparu's life was full and constructive in all ways except one.

This one ordeal that seemed to be a guide to the dizzying heights of self-knowledge, self-confidence and abandoned expression - but only resulted in his feeling more and more 'dotish and babyish'- came packaged in the form of his best friend Sonja.

Sonja had the blessing and the curse of being born a Dougla – father of African descent, mother of Indian. While she could stamp her foot on the ground and proclaim, "Ah is true true Trinbagonian! Dis lan' is mine!" in her constant quest for freedom she couldn't truly portray a mistreated and disadvantaged African slave descendent.

Not a day passed without Sonja preaching that "De chain mus' be broken. De people mus' get up an' make dey voice heard. Dem in Power have tuh be pull down an' trample on. An' de people mus' rule 'cause only de people know wot de people want. An' wot de people want is 'Freedom!' 'Freedom!' An' so long as dey have people in charge, so long as dey have people who want tuh tell yuh wot yuh could do an' cyar do, wot yuh could say an' cyar say, yuh have no 'Freedom!'".

Sonja's focus was totally on 'Faults'. If the eyes look only for faults, the eyes will see many and the mind behind them will provide even more.

This ability to point out where others seemed lacking was the hold that Sonja had on Tuparu. He had a high sense of guilt about his every perceived fault and as such, he held the belief that he had to make himself worthy of Sonja's approval. What Tuparu did not realize was that this ongoing vigilance had created in him a strength that was steadfast, humble and caring which was why Sonja liked him in the first place.

Despite his yearning to please her, it bothered him that no part of her speeches addressed what was right or wrong and most of the principles she protested against were positive in nature and could have been of benefit to the citizens of Trinidad and Tobago.

The Mt. St. George Village Council had planned a 'Good Citizen and Outstanding Family' awards ceremony and the Prime Minister had accepted their invitation to attend and distribute some of the trophies. Now, Sonja's greatest discontent lay with the Prime Minister of Trinidad and Tobago. Nothing the Prime Minister did was acceptable. The moment Sonja heard of this intended attendance, she began making plans to ambush the Prime Minister.

"Wot yuh think, Toop?" she asked Tuparu. "We could put nails in de road an' puncture she tires? Eh? Or we could cut down ah tree an' let it fall just as she passin'? Eh Toop, wot you think? Eh?"

"Who 'We' yuh talking about? Ah not on yuh chupidness. Yuh know dat!" was Tuparu's response.

Sonja started to sweet-talk him, "Aye Tupid Toop, of course is 'We'. Me an' you. We is weebil together. We grow up together. Remember?"

"So wot dat say?" said Tuparu, ready to fight.

"Oh gosh Tuparu boy, yuh know ah cyar do wit'out you. Hush nuh. Yuh always does be telling meh ting tuh make meh feel bad. Why yuh so? Leh we get serious. Wot we go do about dis Prime Minister business?"

"Ah doh know about you but ah have tuh go home now," Tuparu said. Sonja's words had melted his anger. "Ah just remember Mammie did tell meh tuh pick up de fowl egg dem."

"Fowl egg?" Sonja asked thoughtfully.

"Yes, eggs. Yuh know - eggs. De roun' tings dat hens lay; hens dat we call fowls, dus - 'fowl eggs'?"

"Dat's a great idea!" Sonja exclaimed. "Ah always know ah could depend on yuh! Rotten eggs! We go pelt she wit rotten eggs! Yes!"

Tuparu froze in surprise.

"Wot! Wot yuh say? Yuh mad or wot! An' yuh gone back wit dis 'We' ting?"

Sonja was on fire.

"No. No, Toop. Listen. Dat is ah good idea. When dey passin' Blenheim we go pelt dem wit rotten egg so when dey reach Georgia everybody go see wot ah stink Prime Minister dey have! Wot we go do is dis. Yuh know dat bridge by de river-mouth in Blenheim? How it make ah corner? An' it have two more corner before dat as yuh leaving Hope? Well, dey boun' to slow down for dem three corner, so we go hide in de drain by de bridge an' let dem have it dey! Yes! Capital idea!"

Tuparu shook his hands in disagreement, "Not me! Yuh not getting me in dat! An' tuh besides, ah didn' tell you not'ing about pelting rotten egg. Anyway, Ah leaving you an' yuh madness."

Tears sprang to Sonja's eyes, "Please? Please, Tuparu? Come go wit me. Yuh know ah cyar do wit'out you. Yuh is meh backbone. Please, Tuparu? Yuh doh have tuh do not'ing. Jus' be dey wit meh. Please? Jus' promise, please? Oh gosh, dis is ah big thing for meh an' yuh had promise tuh always be dey for meh. Yuh forget dat? Please support meh. Only keep meh company, da's all. Yuh is meh only frien' Tuparu. Yuh know dat! Please?"

"Okay! Okay!" Tuparu gave in. "Okay, Ah'll come wit yuh. But ah not doing not'ing, yuh hear meh? Not'ing!"

Sonja was on top of the world, "Thanks Toop. Oh yes, thanks. Ah'll do everything. Doh worry. Ah'll get de eggs. Make sure dey good rotten. Ah'll pelt dem. Den we go run up in de bush. Nobody go even see we."

"When it is again?" Tuparu asked.

"Is nex' week Saturday, Toop. How yuh could forget somet'ing like that? Yuh brain does surprise meh sometimes. But doh worry, Ah will remin' yuh."

"Sure yuh will," Tuparu muttered, "If not'ing else, Ah sure yuh will."

At 4:30pm on the day of the awards ceremony, Tuparu and Sonja were hidden in the drain on the Blenheim corner before the bridge. Tuparu sat with his back against the side of the drain.

"Anybody could tell meh wot ah doing here? Ah must be de biggest fool in de worl' tuh even be wit'in ah mile ah dis place."

"Toop, check an' see if anybody on de beach or liming under de almond tree an' dem," Sonja whispered.

"No!" Tuparu exclaimed, "No! Ah done tell yuh ah not doing not'ing!"

Sonja flapped her hands, "Hush. Shhhh. Quiet, Toop. Doh hassle yuhself. Yuh wit me. Jus' tuh keep company. Ah'll look, doh worry."

Peeping through the short grass on the edge of the drain, Sonja's eyes darted over the beach to the almond trees and back.

"Okay, Toop. Good. Nobody dey. Dey should be coming anytime now. Ah'll tell yuh when so yuh'll know when tuh run."

Sonja armed herself with four rotten eggs from the dozen or so she had in a small paint-bucket, two in each hand.

"Ah letting dem have it two at ah time. Go be double-barrel shots," she boasted.

"Who go believe my mammie learn meh tuh have better sense dan dis," Tuparu grumbled, "Yuh know wot dis is? Dis is when Mammie does say, 'Frien's does carry yuh but doh bring yuh back!' 'Peer pressure'. Da'is ah nex' word for it."

Sonja looked at Tuparu sitting sorrowfully in the drain.

"Toop. Yuh doh trus' meh?" she asked, "Ah look like ah could ever do anyt'ing tuh hurt yuh? Ah mean, for God sake, is me! Ah know yuh since baby. Ah know over de years we had little fallin' out but ah ever do anyt'ing bad tuh yuh?"

Tuparu squashed himself further into the drain. "Wah about now? Eh? Answer meh. Wah about now?"

As Sonja opened her mouth to answer, it struck her that vehicles were approaching the bridge. A quick look revealed two executive-looking cars accompanied by four motor-cycle escorts.

Sonja sprang up, pelted the eggs and darted out of the drain. Tuparu became aware that something had happened only when he heard Sonja running away.

As he raised himself up to see, a policeman jumped on him and pinned his arms to the ground.

Handcuffs were snapped on his wrists and he was roughly pulled out of the drain. The four policemen who had formed the motorcycle escort surrounded him, three of them with drawn guns.

"Is jus' kids wit rotten eggs," said the policeman who had jumped on Tuparu, "One ah allyuh stay wit meh, de res' go ahead. Who was dat wit yuh?" he asked Tuparu.

Tuparu was in shock and barely breathing. His heart thumped frantically. He had never been so frightened in his life.

The policeman gave him a light slap to revive him. "Catch yuhself, boy. Breathe. Doh drop down on meh now. Who was dat wit yuh?" he asked again.

"Nnn-nnn-nuhbody," Tuparu gasped out.

"Okay. If yuh say so. Yuh big enough tuh do dis, den yuh big enough tuh take wot yuh get. But if was you who pelt dem eggs, yuh does pelt like ah gyurl. De only ting yuh hit was de road. So yuh taking all de blame, eh? Okay. Your funeral. Call ah jeep for dis dangerous terrorist," he told the other policeman who had stayed with him.

During the jeep ride to the police-station and the questioning by the police officers, Tuparu's brain completely locked itself off. Though it seemed that he was being insolent and unresponsive, actually not a thought or emotion of any kind was functioning in his mind.

"Lock him up!" one of the policemen finally said.

Tuparu was taken to an empty cell where the handcuffs were removed and he was shoved in.

CRANNG!

CLANK!

The slamming and locking of the jail door, made of two-inch iron bars, squeezed Tuparu's heart and flipped his stomach.

"Oh God!" he moaned, as realization rushed into him of just where he was, and why.

"Oh God Oh!" he repeated, as he grabbed his belly and sank to the floor.

Tuparu spent that Saturday night, all day Sunday and Monday morning alone. At 10 a.m. on Monday, he was given a change of clothes, handcuffed and escorted to the court-house.

As he stepped into the court-room he saw his family - father, mother, brothers and sisters. At the sight of his mother's tear-stained face, Tuparu's heart twisted and tears flowed freely down his cheeks. The escorting policeman had to guide him to the dock and press his shoulder for him to sit.

Tuparu did not hear a word of anything that was said and couldn't answer anything asked of him. Everything was a blur and the only image in his mind was his mother's face.

After a while, the policeman pulled him up, released the handcuffs and pushed him in the direction of his mother. Tuparu ran to her, grabbed her and starting crying again.

"Ah sorry, Mammie. Ah sorry. Oh gosh, Mammie, Ah sorry," he wept on her shoulder.

"Is okay, Baby, is okay," Tuparu's mother comforted him, "Come leh we go home now. Is okay. We could go home now."

Three weeks afterwards, Tuparu was comfortable with himself and his life was mainly back to normal. He had been fined $1000.00, which his father had paid and which he must repay, given two years community service teaching the tenor pan to primary-school children and also, he had to report to the police-station once a week for the next two years.

Emotionally, Tuparu had matured.

Freedom had sunk its roots in him and was daily growing up with him.

Freedom came after he had wrestled with himself, which is the only war for freedom there is and, Thank God, he won.

The choice of standing firm for what's right and discarding what's wrong is freedom.

The acceptance of knowing and liking oneself is freedom.

The conviction that God is and that on Him one can totally rely is freedom.

Tuparu had often heard his mother say, "Gi' dem one t'ing tuh be confident in an' in everyt'ing, dey go be confident."

His skill on the tenor pan had given him a solid foundation of confidence that contributed to opening his mind and strengthening his purpose. He was now able to accept himself for who he was and to stand firm and strong in his decisions. As written in the Holy Bible, he was now learning to make his 'Yes' mean 'Yes' and his 'No' mean 'No'.

That week, on his way to a session of his community service, he saw Sonja for the first time since she had left him in the drain.

"Aye Toop! Toopie-boy! Ah hear yuh was out," she gushed. "Dem capitalist pigs, dey do any-ting tuh yuh? Dey beat yuh? Dat is dey style. Buh doh worry we go handle dem. Is we. Me an' you an' not'ing dey could do could mash we up!" she finished.

"Not anymore," said Tuparu, and walked away.

Gregory Diaz

Ann-Marie Davis

Born and raised in Signal Hill, Tobago, my love for writing was honed and developed in my teenage years of secondary school, and flourished under the guidance of my English teacher...Mrs Agnes Murray-Thomas. I also seem to have inherited my "mother's writing genes" as she also wrote plays and poems. There is no set time for writing....first, there is a light bulb moment...then thoughts are generated... then ideas race to the fore....next, a structure and distinct pattern become apparent...pen and paper become visible...and what ensues is an eclectic mix of choice words, balanced sequencing and a distinct beat. Writing for me is considered a soothing balm, for my mind, body and soul. I am presently a Foreign Language teacher by profession, and the holder of a BA in Languages/ Linguistics and a Diploma in Education. I also possess diplomas in Journalism, HR Mgt, and Project Mgt. In my free time, I enjoy writing poems and stories, craft, cooking and learning new languages.

A Wasted Life

He seemed intent...in more
ways than one…
To ignore his parents' plea...
For they were aware that the
path he'd tread…
Would be filled with misery.

The advice to...reject evil
friends...
Fell only on deaf ears...
He lived a rather reckless
life...
Throughout his teenaged
years.

He abandoned his role...as a
high school kid...
No sense-he said-it made..
And opted for a life of
crime...
Of which he wasn't afraid.

Until one day...ALAS! Too
late!...
They got the troubling
news...
Their son was killed in broad
daylight...
Soon everyone shared their
views.

Stealing.. killing and
kidnapping...
That was his way of life...
But how could all his parents'
work..
Be blurred by pain and strife?

In utter despair...they sought
advice...
To mend their broken son...
But still he refused any extra
help...
Regardless of what they'd
done.

Their only recourse now
...was to pray...
They lived on bended knee...
And offered up their child to
God...
To be freed from his misery.

The parents were....now
filled with grief...
Their only son was dead...
He died because he refused
to listen....
And was totally misled.

So youths!...beware! Heed all advice...
It is to guide you all...
For if you refuse to accept it now...
You will most surely fall.

Choose friends who will uplift you now...
And encourage you to excel...
For they'll be there through thick and thin...
And assist you to do well.

Have your future plans at hand...
Review them with each day...
Never take your eyes off your goal...
For you will surely stray.

Along life's path....ask for God's grace....
To assist you through it all...
And in the end, you'll emerge a winner....
Standing STRAIGHT and TALL!

Ann-Marie Davis

GOD THE POTTER....YOU THE CLAY

- Life is a mystery to be
  lived....
  Not a problem to be
  solved....
  But some folks just go on
  through life
  With problems
  unresolved.

- God sends us each
  experience....
  As part of his great
  plan....
  And he shapes us and he
  moulds us....
  Just like the potter's
  hand.

- Some people crack under
  the strain....
  And give up right away....
  Others too resist the
  heat...
  And walk another way.

- But some endure the hurt
  and pain...
  And are bent and shaped
  with ease...
  And at the end of all the
  trials...
  God uses them as he
  please.

- And so it is you know a
  man...
  By the mettle from which
  he's made...
  He can endure the tests
  of life...
  His strength can never
  fade.

- He takes each trial one by
  one...
  And treats it, not with
  fear…
  And knows throughout
  the stress of life...
  His loving God is there.

- God holds you up, and
  wipes your tears....
  And he will see you
  through...

And he will bring you to
that place...
Where you can start
anew.

- So as you watch your
  Lord at work...
  With vessels big and
  small...
  He has both there...the
  weak and strong....
  And he moulds and
  shapes them all.

- Which one are you...you
  may still ask....
  The weak one or the
  strong?
  To crack under the
  intense heat.....

Or last out now real
long?

- Lord...as you mould your
  vessels now.....
  Into the shape you
  choose.....
  Help me always be that
  strong.....
  And not a chance to lose.

- So mould me Lord and
  shape me, Lord.....
  Into a brand new soul.....
  And in the end, I know
  I'll be...
  Purified as gold!

Ann–Marie Davis

THE KINDNESS TREE

- Be kind to all, both big
  and small,
  Be kind in word and
  deed,
  What's needed is a tiny
  act,
  Small as a mustard seed.

- You plant this very
  minute seed,
  In the garden that's called
  Life,
  You weed it round, and
  tend to it,
  And uproot weeds of
  strife.

- You watch it daily
  blossom now,
  Into the kindness tree,
  And then you pluck a leaf
  or two
  And sit right back and
  see.

- Both leaves represent
  kindness

  A good deed done
  someday,
  It may be offering words
  of cheer,
  Or showing them the
  way.

- You pluck more leaves
  from this great tree,
  And cheer someone who's
  ill,
  And share with those
  who are in need,
  And surely do His will.

- And as all the days just
  come and go,
  And leaves become much
  less,
  You strive to be really
  kind to all,
  Recognizing you are
  blessed.

- And when the last leaf is
  then plucked,
  Another good deed is
  done,

Rest assured you're on
your way,
To winning that glorious
crown.

- And now the tree is stark
and bare,
Without a leaf in sight,
You start the process once
again,
And continue to do
what's right.

- And so you plant a seed
again,
Sit back and watch it
grow,
And as the leaves slowly
emerge,
Kindness acts will follow.

Ann-Marie Davis

$\mathcal{M}$ilca Robinson Reid

MILCA ROBINSON REID – Her beginnings as a writer were driven by her desire to change people's negative perceptions of her. She declares that writing has allowed her life "to bloom in another direction". Out of all the adversities that she faced, she emerged victorious and the world has now been presented with an educational psychologist, educator, lecturer, teacher, counsellor, social worker, guidance officer, researcher, visual artist, performing artist, playwright, poet, hall and cake decorator, cricketer, netballer, master of ceremonies and judge (competitions).

Milca has been composing songs, poems, stories and plays since she was nine years of age. She attended the University of the West Indies – Mona and St Augustine campuses –where she graduated with a Certificate in Mathematics Education and a Bachelor's degree in Educational Administration. She later obtained a Master of Arts degree in Educational Psychology from Andrews University. She has been responsible for training several school principals and teachers in Mathematics Education in Grenada and Trinidad and Tobago. As a teacher of Developmental Math, Drug Administration and Psychology at COSTAATT she achieved record passes. She also lectured at the University of the West Indies (U.W.I), the University of the Southern Caribbean (U.S.C) and the University of Trinidad and Tobago (U.T.T) in varied fields. Her distinguished academic accomplishments equipped her with critical skills in Psychological Testing, Research, Statistics, and Counselling. She is a member of The American Psychological Association and Trinidad and Tobago Association of Psychologists.

She has always been a community person and a member of several NGOs. She has served as President, Secretary and Treasurer of the Calder Hall Community Councils; President and Secretary of Gaylords Sports and Cultural Club; Captain of Gaylord's traditional cricket team; Secretary of The Tobago Women's Cricket Association; Vice President of THANKS, Secretary of the Tobago Writers' Forum and Vice President of The Tobago Writers Guild.

CRIME
(Milca Robinson Reid)

I
Am crime
I'm called Criminal,
With Violence on my mind,
I can instigate any
And carry down many.
I respect no race,
No colour, no age.
Ethnicity, class, religion,
Height or wealth,
Only
DEATH
Yes,
Death is
My only gain,
But, it is your pain,
As I seduce not in vain.
All my selections can't get away,
Obey, they must,
And hit the
Dust.
I
Employ
The angry,
Lazy and Greedy
I hang out with addicts,
Bandits, rapists

Alcoholics, murderers, shop lifters,
In fact they are
My Dearest
And Best
Friends.
So
Beware,
Stay far from me,
You have time to spare?
Find a Positive Peer,
Do a puzzle,
Play scrabble.
Sing, dance, read or
Peddle.
I,
Spare none,
I love guns,
I adore knives,
And all other weapons
If you have any
YOU, are my DESTINY,
I'll cause you to kill,
I'll cause you to hate,
I'll cause you to steal,
I'll cause you to rape.
So leave the razors,
The scissors, knives and guns
Be a hero,
A visual artist

A
Bookworm
Say
No to guns
Say No, No to drugs,
Say no to Me and alcohol,
Run from me, Stay away from me,
Say yes to school, books values,
Take up the tools,
Play pan, sing calypso,
Rap and soca,
Please!
Stop crime.
Live,
Don't die
Don't let your loved ones cry
Don't cause any more to die,
Hear Me! When I say
Crime pays no one
Crime cares for no one,
Feels no pain, brings no gain,
Does not go to jail.
Crime wants you DEAD,
To push you in the
Ground.
Live
Be Positive
Obey your parents
Get an Education,
What about electrical installation,

Carpentry, masonry, plumbing, sewing
Then, there is athletics,
There is bread making,
Decorating,
Agriculture
And
Sports
Learn
Today,
Education is important.
Crime does not pay,
Begin your tomorrow
By starting today.

HERITAGE BEGINNINGS
Authored by Milca Robinson Reid

What was that I sat and heard abusing my mind?
As I sat viewing the programme Rise and Shine?
That was not the only occasion it was aired on Television.
In fact it was the third I experienced that intrusion,
The hosts' incessant repetition – Heritage Festival is Dr. Elder's brain child.
And viewers endorsing and twisting the argument of its origin.

Dr. J. D. Elder was a reputable author,
Such a decent, respectable luminary I can't imagine would have plagiarized.
Did he ever lay claim to this hideous, intellectual property act?
Did he truly plagiarize, or was it to him entrusted?
Or was the intent to obfuscate the fact?
Was it for fame, wealth or political aggrandizement?
Or, bare-faced bias, revenge or maliciousness?

What ever the reason, please, if you are an instigator, follower, or mischief maker, think again.
Please refrain and consider what this poet has to offer on this sordid situation.
In my opinion, It is imperative that after you have witnessed this rendition, that you joggle your conscience.
Eliminate bias and or prejudicial thinking and as you read this factual account, do your own analysis, interpretation and the ultimate evaluation before you ignorantly internalize a position.

At a significant event, in the year nineteen eighty four,
One Sunday, at Shaw Park's Cultural stage for sure,
Tobago's Youths and other invited groups
Converged in that rustic pavilion.
The writer was community representative at that function,
To commemorate "World Youth Day International"

Two speakers did me impress, Supervisor of Community
Development -Lydia Paul
And Assembly Man George Stanley Beard, Assistant Secretary
for Education, Tourism and Culture.
Lydia presented her vision to keep the communities together
and elevate our culture
Invited all interested to meet her, to form a mass island wide
folk choir
On Wednesday of that same week, at her office on Bacolet Street.
In the antiquated edifice - The Scarborough Community Centre.

Secretary Beard voiced his own thoughts to show case Tobago's
Culture.
Predicated on a foreign experience, he shared, a modified
version could be staged here.
Each village must stage its own affair to package a Cultural
Theatre far and near
If we don't, it will disappear. An excellent way to attract tourists
here,
And a methodology for preservation of our culture
Together with the added benefit of an economic booster,
There is no better way to embrace and sustain our ancestors'
venture.

In a thinking- on -the -spot mannerism, he promulgated,
Moriah is the best locale for Ole Time Wedding!
Other communities will suggest their surroundings.
A definite way to enhance our economy,
And imprint Tobago internationally.
The crowd was silent as a door nail, as cool as cucumber and
as though in slumber.
My hopes were dashed, as I anticipated an applaud
Just then, the wind had a voice as it gave a slight roar.

The following week, my decision I activated.
I hastened on foot to join the choir.
As an ardent Performing Arts lover and player
I positioned myself at the Scarborough centre.
With that choir leader, Mr. King we had a very good director.,
I can still recall Lydia's facial, expression of cheer as the
announcer.
Yet, I left there that night, my expectations dashed, and a
resolution never to go back.
As the intent was obscured or deviated from prior advertisement.

The first episode from the introductory package
Was indeed "The Moriah Ole Time Wedding."
The fulfillment of Assistant Secretary Beard's suggested first Act
His vision was brought to the fore with the initiation at Shaw
Park,
The Moravian Hall provided a sanctuary
In which the couple received their blessing
Sardines with pomp and pride doned, in ole time frocks and
stone crushers

Beaver hats, scissors tail, frills and flowers
Snugly packed in wooden pews and no space to witness history.
Inside bursting and, joining the churchyard's periphery.

The road became a thoroughfare, vendors, dancers, musicians galore
Young and old, quick and lame made their way to the centre hall
To view and participate in pageantry -the reception ball.
The procession moved in brush back style, 2 steps forward, 3 steps backward,
In my opinion this was methodological simulation.
Cause If 2 is forward and 3 is backward, after two back steps the third is stop
Ole time subtle way of love consummation.

To each one a gift was given, according to God's judgment and prerogative.
Whereas some use it to give God glory, others use it for fame and easy money,
While some use it for self development, the visionary used his for development of country,
Why keep his covered, yet laud it on another,
I pray that we respect the wisdom of Stanley, and after
------years of Heritage on the calendar,
It's time to reward and give him lost honour.
Bless the work of his mind and reward him in kind.

Tobago Indigenous Art Form
Penned by Milca Robinson Reid

Wake up people wake up! Wake up people wake up.
Those are the sounds that greeted the ear
 In the still of the dark nights of that era.
That made adults quiver and children cower
Peeping from under the cover with pounding hearts
To seek shelter from the pending news that heralded, DEATH.
Once somebody dead, that unwanted refrain was heard again, and again.
Cause 'twas that refrain was the only way to let Tobagonians know, somebody dead again.
With it all, everyone knew that after that unwelcomed episode,
Came the prelude to the exit ceremony the all encompassing Wake!
Yuh see, Trini's hook on to Carnival fete, but Wake is wah we ketch and kept.
For me, Wake is ah we thing, though the death announcement was frightening.
Yuh see, it's a time fuh total unity, sympathy and keeping company
As the religious, whether Friday, Sabbath or Sunday worshippers
In fellowship, we Wake together.

Once somebody dead, from Crown Point, L'anse fourmi or Charlotteville,
Yuh free to attend, even if not invited.
An hear nuh, yuh nah ha fu pay,

but yuh can kerry a bottle a rum, puncheon, or a bunch ah green fig.
A pan a crix, a tray a sweet bread even a bath pan ah loaf, or box a hops bread.
Yuh can go with sandwich, fish, even a bundle ah wood or cash liquid
Anything is welcome to cover the helava funeral expense.

Yuh ent ha fu do nothing in the Wake.
Yuh feel to lip sinc? Sing
Yuh feel to dance? Prance
Yuh feel to laugh, do so till yuh cry.
However, yuh could eat free and participate in ole talk,
Man or woman talk, straight talk, bad talk, gossip, politics.
With anyone or all who yuh deem fit.
The biggest act ah the gathering is singing sankies, choruses and hymns
Accompanied by casio, mouth organ, even tambourine.
Bottle an spoon, timberlee four and six string.
An we cyah leave out the drumming part,
Together with hand clapping to provide rhythm.
That ah, ah we heritage,
Come all the way from Africa Land,
Let us preserve this heritage in ah ah we package.
Who wan to tap? Tap! just tap
Who want to rap? Rap just Rap
If yuh want to help the chairman,
Sing Doh, Ti, Lah, Soh, Fah, Meh, Ray, Doh !

The singing must have a leader.

They label he Mr. Chairman.
He does sit down at the head a the table,
Looking over he spectacle,
He calls some song, starts some songs, controls the order and
each note
Doh, tih, lah, soh, fah, me, ray, doh, If the singers allow him
to do so.
Cause there is much competition to be choir master.
Every song book is in attendance.
New Day, Christ In Song, Seven Days, Old and New, Anglican.
Baptiste Church Hymnal, Methodist an Moravian.
The musicians play in any rhythm,
Dirge, folk, socca, reggae, calypso or bele.
Regardless of wha, the mourners belch them out right.
Now and again ih geh big argument,
To tek over the leader's position,
And prevent anyone song book taking prominence.
But even if ih have dissention we end in the same position,
SING.

Wake nuh singing one.
It have them who play card by the side.
Men trying to heng one another Jack.
While some hoard the King or Queen from every pack.
Some settle fuh 10 ah spade, club, heart or diamaid
Yet others prize Ace as TRUMP.
If yuh listen good tonight yuh goh hear ah Jack Dead
Or a scream, indicating a player won.
All around the yard groups chat.
Two by two, three by three even five six and groups of seven.

They does call any number, talk anything, and everything,
As a matter ah fact, the dead play a big part in all ah that.
 Cause when deh ready they even talk the dead.
Yuh talk all you know and whe you ent know bout it.
Sometimes yuh does wonder, if is the same dead yuh did know.
When it nearing midnight, the mourners belch out,
Bring it, Mr. Chairman bring it, bring it with a willing heart.
As if to say that is wha they come for.
They does goh down in they baratone, semitone, heavy tone
and then, AMEN

THE UNINVITED INVITED GUESTS

The Occasion is a birthday party. Expected twenty five invitees
only
When I did catch my self, only uninvited guests attended.
The first to come was comessive Greeta, who happened to be
my next door neighbour.
Put her self by the side door. Her name is Greeter, sh'd meet
and greet all.
The next to come was my sister, she came with her husband and
her partner,
And the partner brought his old partner and another. I cyah
understand our people at all.
By the time Greeta settled down, I saw Teena, heading towards
the front,
Greeta shout out, "Hi Teena, look me deh here, Come by the
side doh, it better here than there."
''Leave the front doh for the dignataries, the spike heels and
the big wigs,
Leh we lime by this side doh, every now an then we goh slip
in fuh the Show!"
''Greeta, please don't do me that. Teena leave! Can you please
go back?
I catered for twenty five only celebreties, Carnival time would
be your festivity."
"Carnival who? well tonight goh be the real Carnival. With
Talibut and Taliman the party goh be real nice along with
Bucaneers and Katzen Jammers.
Them two just waiting on a call to bring dey side, bottle,
spoon an iron."

"Aa, Aa, Teena, look! look Talibut ah come, he an he big, big, son."

"Talibut! Talibut! nah fuh pass deh, everybody down here. Teena, me an the birthday gual,"

"Like she guests and them nah ah come. Ah we ha fuh bail she out, and tek shame out she mouth."

"Teena, what kina drink you have deh? Yuh know ah does drink puncheon,

An look, me partner Taliman ah come. He, ih patner Stellone, Stallone keep woman an she man fren."

", gih yuh boy Talibut ah dance." "Nah, Nah, Nah Teena, yuh cyah do that, Yuh cyah wine first Is Miss Piety Party."

"Party wha, an none ah she people them nah reach yet? So wait nah, we must just stand up here just so?"

"An besides, who know who invited from who is guest? She too pompous with sheself."

"We goh be the ones to dine an wine.. Tonight we goh be more than honoured guests."

"Buh Miss Piety, yuh know it long after twelve. Whey you specially invited and them?"

Whey Miss Sobriety, Miss Dainty and Miss My Fair Lady? Ms. Charity, Chief Sec, Minority Leader and Pit? Whey Delmon and Nella, What mek all ah them nah dey here? To celebrate with you Miss Vanity Fair."

"Girl, I'm really, surely disappointed. It' s way after midnight and none of them is in sight."

Not even my MC and his fiancée. Just now, night will appear and sun blaze down its light."

"Piety guyl, nah worry bout that, we will erase your shame, and keep you sane."

"My gosh! What would I do now? My caterers have not me disappoint, Look, she just pull up at the front!"

Their job is to serve and share, and my perceived friends haven't shown.

My desire is everyone would sit and dine, eat, drink and lime in fine style.

With no one to seat, drink and eat, no fan fair, no chit chat but embarrasment slight, very soon sun light will peak with all its might."

"Piety, so wha ah we so be? Although we are unwanted invitees we can occupy a seat each,

Bucaneers, Jammers will over fill the chairs and you wouldn't have to worry bout guests to be served."

"Oh my gosh, What is this? Current gone? What a disgusting situation!"

"Piety, somebody like you must have a back up? Goh put on yuh delco. T&Tec cyah keep we in this mess fuh long. Bring the delco leh we have we fun. Is now self we ah yuh real chums."

"Taliman, whey yuh going wid the bucket in ah the dark?

"Teena shut you rusty man trap. We goh meet in the front."

"Greeta, current come back, look in a meh bag an pass me apron. Since orlier ah night, she shoulda sorve snack pack. Taliman gone wid the souse, me ah goh wid the snack packs."

Moder oh, Look Piety ah come. Piety, leh go yuh self, fine style or awkward wine, yuh is still Miss Pomp and Pride and we forever your faithful frens. Bring out everything, meats, treats anything.

Leh ah we eat, drink and be merry. After all, ah we ah one. Me mumma ah fuh you father sista. We from the same ordinary family tree.

FISH VENDOR

Come! Geh yuh fish!
An go cook a nice dish.
Geh yuh cavalee, groupa, bonito,
Red fish, king fish, albaco.

Jessica, wha mek yuh tek me fish an yuh nah want to pay me
fuh it?
Because yuh daughter pregnant fuh me son,
Is no reason wha mek me must pay fuh yuh fish
Me nuh obligated to you an she one bit.

Look woman, wha the hell me haf to do wid who yuh owe
from who yuh ent owe?
Yuh know how much hell ah does ketch wid me fish?
Yuh know how much ah does pay fuh it?
Try give me me money before ah explode.

Come gyal! Come geh yuh fish,
 An goh cook a nice dish.
Cook steam fish, fry fish, oil down fish,
Curry fish, roast fish, corn fish, even stew fish.

Wait nah, ah who tell Jessica the baby ah fuh me son?
Time nah ah wait pan no man, baby soon ah come.
Just wait till the baby mek its appearance,
Only then she goh know who is the male parent.

Today over slow, look how much fish me still have here.
An the multitude ah flies ent making it easier.
The more me fan, the more they come wrong
An lak ah if they want to knock me down.

Keskereng he have me real tie up,
Ten spirits to mek me business buss,
The more ah fan fly, the more they multiply,
Little bit more, ah me they goh strike..

Come geh yuh fish, goh cook a nice dish.
Jessica, yuh nah here whey me say?
Me son nah haf fuh mind yuh daughter,
Leh she goh look for another father.

Little gyall, how much an wha kind ah fish yuh want ?
Leh me weigh this one here fuh yuh.
Yuh nah sure if it fresh an which one to tek?
They come direct from the sea to me. Yuh ent see how they
wet?

Anyway, Yuh mumma an me ah good frens,
Leh me give she a good bargain.
When she want fresh fish, she head straight to fuh me stall.
This one a goh keep real fresh, me fix it up nice wid salt.
Yuh goh kerry this home give she,
it can mek a nice fish broff or fish tea.
The extra fish is wha she gain,
Because me nuh ha no change

Tell me whe yuh mean by the eye sink in?
Yuh nah see the fish dead, it can no longer see again?
Tek this, and go home straight before it too late.
Yuh hear darling, nuh keep she ah wait.

But hear tha little wretch, bout the fish eye sink in.
Them young people ent know they little place.
Wha the france she know bout condition or kind ah fish?
She mumma go haf fuh tek the George Renking.

Red fish, antrovi, barracuta, snapper,
Carite, shark bonito, big jacks.
Come you deh, come an geh yuh fish.
Kerry it home an cook any dish.

Miss Scoby darling yuh look nice this morning,
Me spirit tell me that yuh coming.
An ah keep this one fuh you and Abel,
and that one to prepare fuh you clientele.
What! You want Cavalie?
Me ent nah hah no cavalie.
Fish is still fish, By what ever name, all ah the same.
They smell the same, and they dwelling is the same.

An how the france ah go get any sale if me nah call all the names.
Every morning me stan up by the road, all them drivers does pass
me full load.
Who have space drive at a zooming pace,
Yuh swear they late for heaven's gate.

They nah know Zilla, Ioana an Lillian tell me what mek they nah a stop,
What mek they does pass me like full bus.
They say me bath pan does tek up the whole car trunk,
and me buttocks does spread out in front.

Or, it does occupy the whole back seat.
So soon as they see me, deh does rev up full speed.
They say me weight does buss up seat spring, an ah does smell like manderine.
And whenever ah take me exit, the vehicle smell like smoke herring.

When everyone pay fuh travelling, me haf to pay for signalling stop.
Me pay fuh attention and sitting,
Me pay for excess flesh, the pan and the stink.
And some mek me even pay for flat tire and broken spring.

Ah really wuk hard today, but ah ent mek much money either.
Is Keskereng ah have to blame,
Like he spirits ent really lame,
An they know how to play the game.

Well me can play the game better.
Leh him wait till later,
Me only ah wait till it is night time,
To sail him out of sight in ah me bath pan.

$\mathcal{L}$aureen Burris-Phillip

LAUREEN BURRIS-PHILLIP was born in Scarborough TOBAGO, schooled at Scarborough Methodist Primary and Bishop Anstey High School, Port of Spain, Trinidad, the University of the West Indies, St. Augustine and the University of Wisconsin, Madison in the United States.

Her areas of study were agriculture and agricultural economics. She is interested in Writing, Music, Dress Design, and Woodwork. Laureen was the Commonwealth Short Story winner for this region in 1996 for "Mammy's Harangue" and received an honourable mention in the Writers' Digest Annual competition in 1997 for submission in the area of Children's non-fiction.

She was married to Gerald Phillip, deceased, and has two adult daughters, a chef/economist/art historian and a budding lawyer/political scientist.

She is a Christian, and in spite of the vicissitudes of life, a happy person.

****

MAMMY'S HARANGUE

(1996 Commonwealth Short Story winner for the Region)
Laureen Burris-Phillip

"Oho, so you is a big woman now! I can't talk to yuh! Yuh feel yuh going secondary school an' yuh bright and I don't know nutten. Well let me tell yuh somet'ing. I know enough to bring you to this age of fourteen without anything bad happening to yuh! Yuh feel that fourteen is adult? I have news fuh you! Fourteen is chile still. Not little chile but still child. And if necessary I'll break in yuh tail!"

The truth is that I never like to hit and beat. I always feel ah could reason wit' yuh and find other ways to discipline. But sometimes I feel them ole people was right. Anytime alyuh slip, is to let you have it, then and there.

I get plenty licks in full view of my friends because my mother used to say, NO CHILE ain't embarrassing her in public. But I never do you dat because I know how I used to be so shame.

One day, the teacher write a note home to say that I misbehaving in class. When I carry home de note, my mother din say anything. The next day, that lady take a taxi and come up in school to beat me. That is how people used to discipline children long time.

Times change and I feel a mother have to treat her chile with respect. BUT the chile have to respect the mother too. I might not be able to chat no French to you or discus Portia speech from Shakespeare, but I still bring you in this world and take care ah yuh when you couldn't help yuhself. And in case you didn't notice, I still putting food on the table. When yuh start feeling uppity, remind yuhself ah dat.

When I give you ah instruction, I expect you to obey. All this questioning is not necessary. Alyuh get that from television! All dem foreign people doan train their children properly at all. And they infecting the whole world by putting that bad behaviour on TV, as if that is anything for people to follow.

The books they making now is just as bad. Only murder mystery and obeah occult stupidness. Longtime books used to build character. Yuh mind is a precious thing! Yuh can't be filling it up with no junk!!! But again, alyuh feel alyuh know everything. Ah warning yuh, doan lemme see them stupid books in here again.

And as for you room! Yuh feel as is your room, yuh could keep it any way yuh want. But this is still my house and yuh have to abide by my rules as long as you live here. I doan want no pigsty because I aint minding no pig! Right! So yuh better go and tidy up that room right now.

Furthermore, doan be asking me for no expensive clothes with people name on it. Who de hell is Carl Mackee? And why yuh should wear his jeans? He is not yuh fadder!! You will get decent, proper clothes that I could afford and doan tell me no foolishness 'bout designer clothes.

And de next ting, when yuh fadder come by here to see you, yuh will answer him properly. He never marry me but that is between me and he. So you doan get involve in dat!! As a matter a fack, I glad now I ain't married because no man in this house to confuse me so I could concentrate on you!

So stop pushing out yuh mout' at me and go an' wash up them wares in de sink, YUH HEAR!!!!!

One Angry Woman
Laureen Burris-Phillip

There is the sound of police whistles and a commotion outside as if many people are running. Then "she" comes running through the door with a broken umbrella.

She runs onto the stage, breathless, dishevelled and looking over her shoulder all the time.

"They come fuh me but ah get away. Yuh remember me from de last time? Is I who ask alyuh whey alyuh watching. But ah din have time to tell the full story. Ah have a little girl. If you see she, she is a real sweetie. Real sweet. An ah trying with her because I really don't want her in dis kind a life. She eight. So ah sending her to piano lessons and ah little dancing. Yuh know dat does help wid de walking.

"You doesn't notice how dem girls in town walking. Backside stick out; everyting swinging from side to side. Like de ole time calypso. Yuh remember it?

(Sing and Demonstrate)   *"Chest jumping, behind bumping*

They walking in saga ting,
jest because they want to spend mih dollars!!"

"HA ha, dem young people eh know dat one at all!!!"

"But I want she to walk proper. Yuh know how dey use to tell you long time. Walk tall, stand tall and sit tall. Swing the leg from the hip when walking. Walk the line. Put a big book on yuh head and balance. So ah trying!!

"But yuh know yuh have to talk with yuh children and listen to them carefully. She really mention a man who does be hanging round by the dance school. So I tell her ask de dance teacher, ask him what he doing there. She tell me he does be dong de road where de teacher can't see him. So I pick up on dat one time. I tell her to wait for me I will come and pick her up early today. But yuh know how children harden. So I go down there earlyish to see wha really goin on. "As I round the corner by de school, I look dong de road, see my chile, this man holding her han and pulling her along and de other children running off.

"Well, I fly dong de road and ah hit he one lash wid dis umbrella here. He leggo my chile hand and ah push she behind me and he tun rong and raise he hand. Who tell he do dat. I connect wid de umbrella again and den another one to he foot by de knee. He went down and ah give him two more. And ah take me chile and ah take off. But ah feel de police might be coming for me so ah drop she off by my aunt and I run down here. And de police behind me fuh truth. Dat must be 21st century policing. Dey reach real quick!!! When you call dem for real crime dey coming two hours afta but if is little stupidness they reach fas fas fas!!!

"But I eh sorry yuh know. Ah ent sorry at all!!! I only sorry I din give him two more. Because what a big man so harassing little children for? He sick!!! The community should step in to help and if necessary show disapproval. Let dem kina men get treatment!! Injection, and whatever.

"And alyuh know it have some mudders doesn't study dese things at all. Somebody advantaging your chile and you have nothing to say or do!!! How dat could be? Children ain't ask us to come here. We have to protect them. And dese days we have to look out fuh de girls and de boys.

"And de fadders!!! Fadders suppose to be the main protector of dere family. That is why when you go out, yuh usually going out with a fella!!! He suppose to protect yuh!!! I doan know what really goin on dese days. Dem men and dem they want to have children with Jean, Janet and Jasmine. Dem lady aint good enough to married but they could be yuh children mother. So yuh doan like yuh children, yuh hate dem!!! Steups!!!

"Well dat is alyuh. Let the record show dat, I aint making no joke. I stanning up for mine as bes I could. An you see in school, I hear de problem is real. So yuh know I does haunt de school. I always up dey talking to the teacher. I doan care if they vex and every day me and mi chile chatting. I want to know everything dat goin' on in dere. Plenty people does know tings that goin on and dey doan say nutten. But you ever think that you may be there to protect your children now but who goin protect yuh grandchildren? Because ignoring it now means the problem eh going away. So if when you old and feeble, something happen to yuh granchile, how you going to feel? Eh? Answer me dat!!! I doan know, I doan know, but I trying mih best."

The whistles start again and she grabs up her umbrella and her bag and says,

"Hmm. Dey coming again!! Ah ha to run. If dey ask alyuh tell dem a gorn down so. Ah gorn!!!"

GROWING UP RED

In the Caribbean, "red" means any of the varying shades of skin colour caused by the mixing of the people of African descent and the Caucasian people. In the barbaric days of slavery, the unscrupulous colonizers promoted the idea of classes of the enslaved based on skin colour. The idea being that the closer you are in colour to the so-called "master race" the better you were. Thus the lighter the skin colour the more acceptable you were. And there was the corollary of the hair, since the lighter the skin colour, generally the straighter the hair. And naturally straight hair was, and still is, deemed to be better than the natural hair of the West African.

Different terminologies were developed to express all the above ideas of difference. There is the mulatto, with refinements like octoroon, browning, brown skin, fair skin, light skin with darkie, black skin, blackie or even a nickname "Quarter Past Midnight" (meaning so black that you are blacker than midnight) on the other end of the spectrum to describe the varying shades of mixture and colour. The interesting thing is that there are adjectives that over time have become associated with the differing descriptions. So you hear a "nice fair skin girl with the pretty hair" or a "black ugly girl with hard hair". Another very piquant phrase is a "pretty darkie"; always said with a little surprise in the voice since everyone knows that darkie and blackie cannot possibly be pretty under normal circumstances.

The dislike of their skin colour is so great in some people that there is a thriving business in "bleach" cream which contains chemicals which lighten the skin. This is a trend seen in many popular entertainers who are apparently of the view that they look better with paler skins. The chemicals in bleach cream are known to be dangerous and damaging to the skin.

Hair has been mentioned but there is a whole vocabulary attached to hair. The more African type hair is described as "hard head, nappy, rough, tough, uncontrollable as opposed to smooth and shiny, straight and soft, that is apparently the way *"hair is supposed to be."* So there is a great income generating business in "weaves", that is human hair or synthetic hair that is sewn or stuck into track plaits on the head of the recipient, thus producing the effect of "nice, long, soft hair." Or there is always the alkaline hair relaxing (straightening) process or the old time hot comb. All this is in the attempt to have soft, straight hair.

These and other throwbacks from the unfortunate days of slavery still plague us today. One of the very obvious but not discussed aspects of this is the sense of entitlement that many people who are lighter coloured have. Essentially they have found themselves in a privileged place; lighter skinned girls are considered better looking and seem to have more advantages, more license than other girls. It seems that they are in some way more valuable than their darker skinned sisters. This does not operate in exactly the same way for young men although, even for them, it's better to be a lighter colour. Thus for a lighter skinned girl, the boyfriend would be more willing to compromise on most issues. Many young men indicate that they are not too keen on the darker skinned girls and describe them in very negative ways.

In Trinidad and Tobago, all of the above is further complicated by the fact that a significant number of our citizens are of East Indian descent.

This is all very sad! It is a perpetuation of the attitudes associated with slavery in an almost self-destructive way. It should be considered, given the behaviour of the "slave owners" that the lighter the colour the closer the rape of our race. Many people do not think of these matters. They accept the world as they find it and therefore use the bleaching cream, sew on the hair and hope for the best. If our people are to develop a strong sense of our self-worth which is really essential for any real development to take place, we have to confront these issues; they have to be ventilated and discussed. We have to get to a place where for the majority of people in this country, black is fine, fair skin is fine, white is fine, nappy is fine and straight is fine.

$\mathcal{D}$eborah Moore-Miggins

DEBORAH MOORE-MIGGINS was born in Bethel, Tobago. She credits her village and "Teacher" Euline Isaac, deceased, for her deep love of culture, especially mas, the speech band and the steel pan – all of which she played at an early age.

Her love of writing began with her love of and curiosity about words. This love was nurtured from the several recitations she was called upon to perform from the time she was a toddler, in her Moravian Church. It continued with her composition of several speeches and winning calypsoes for herself and family members. Her description in this book about how a speech band is produced compels the conclusion that she has composed numerous speeches for the speech band.

An Attorney at Law by profession, she confesses to a fascination with old time stories and sayings which she calls 'proverbs'. She insists that Tobago has more than its fair share of these witty and profound words of wisdom. In 2006 she published the book called "The Caribbean Proverbs that Raised us".

CHARLIE LEITH - THE TOBAGO SPEECHBAND PIONEER

(Excerpt from the soon-to-be published book of the same name)

Deborah Moore-Miggins

1. A MAN OF WORDS IS BORN

Most times when a great person is born he or she comes into the world quietly and no one knows that something momentous has just occurred. Except in the case of Jesus Christ, few people know that a new born baby is destined to do something exceptional in his own peculiar way.

Even the mother of that baby rarely knows or realizes that she has given birth to a child whose name would be on the lips of everyone in his or her community, his or her country or the world, for a long time even after his or her death. The man Charles Leith of Bethel Village, Tobago, was such a child. He was more familiarly known among his villagers as "Charlie Leith".

Charlie Leith was the pioneer of the speech band art form in Tobago. No, he was a legend of the art form. He is indisputably the person who was almost solely responsible for the speech band being so developed that it now stands as one of the ways by which Tobago's oral traditions are identified on the international scene.

Those who know the story of the Tobago speech band and those who are today moved to uncontrollable laughter and enjoyment by some of the witty and humorous speeches delivered by speech band members, cannot help but feel awe and wonderment at the man, Charlie Leith who was born in such humble circumstances.

How could such an ordinary man become so visionary in his outlook and be so persistent in his attitude? How does he grow to become so dedicated to an idea, so clear in his mind that he was on to something extra-ordinary with the speech band, that he would commit himself to it with such intensity?

How does one, who was born into virtual poverty as he and his fellow villagers were, at that time, understand what it takes to produce an art form that would make a difference in the lives of the people of Tobago and define their very existence as Tobagonians?

These are very compelling questions that one has to ask when considering the Tobago speech band and its pioneers. Certainly the parents of Charlie Leith did not have a clue at the time of his birth about the immense talent that would emerge from this small infant. They did not know that when he exited life's stage some 80-odd years later he would leave an entire island responding with joy and sheer excitement to the Tobago speech band.

Charlie Leith, whose legal name was Charles Emmanuel Leith, was born in Lower Bethel in the small Island of Tobago on the 10th day of March, 1902. He was the child of Rosetta Leith, formerly Charles, but little is retained about his father.

Rosetta, like almost everyone in Tobago in those years, was called by a "home name" or "village name", and her "home name" was "Gran Milkie". What it meant or why she was so called is a mystery to those who came afterwards but that was the name by which she was known in her community of Bethel.

Charlie himself was to earn several nicknames in his life all of which reflected his wide and varied life experiences. Names such as "Chum", "Cane Peeling", "Buck Shoe", "Pitch Oil" and "Master Driver" all referred to that one loveable person known as Charlie Leith.

His daughter, Merle Phillips, born Merle Leith, says that as far as she knows there was nothing in Charlie's young life which foretold the fact that he would grow up to be the speech band pioneer that he became. She said that she never saw him write a speech, practise it or utter one under his breath like most speech band practitioners do today when fine-tuning their speeches. Also she has never heard that as a young man he excelled at poetry or essay writing or such thing. Charlie Leith simply felt a passion for the speech band in his young adult years and from then he nurtured this passion to the hilt.

The young Charles Leith grew up in Bethel as any other normal young man pursuing activities such as making and playing top, toy cars and roller and sliding downhill on a branch from a tall tree that is called a "cabbage tree". It is said that he showed an uncanny ability to repair mechanical things. He made and repaired wooden box carts, rollers and toy cars which the boys of that time used to race each other.

Had he the opportunity there is no doubt he would have become an excellent builder or mechanical engineer.

At some time during his early adult life Charlie went to Trinidad to earn his living. His experiences there would later be reflected in many of his speeches in the speech band. He liked to use a line about *"going down de main, in the city of Port of Spain"*. He, however, returned to Tobago while still a young man and obtained a job as a bus driver, produced a family and lived out the rest of his life in Tobago where he perfected the Tobago art form known as the speech band.

2. DRAG YUH BOW, MR. FIDDLER!

What does one say about the Tobago speech band that has not yet been said? For me, it is a masterful piece of storytelling, oratory if you wish, which is delivered with wit, humour and good ole Caribbean picong. All this to the accompaniment of some sweet tambourine music spicing up the presentation. In the old days the speech band would come out once per year at Carnival time as it was essentially a Carnival band. There were usually about eight or nine members in the band and they danced and pranced on the stage but mainly they gave speeches about current affairs or village jokes and rumours.

Unless the speech rhymes, however, it is not speech band. Unless it carries that witty and dramatic punch line at the end, it just is not speech band. And unless it is on a topic which is familiar to the audience, or to which they can relate, it ain't speech band, either.

You see, a good speech never really identifies by name the person to whom the speaker is referring. A good speechifier would present the speech so skillfully that the audience is able to figure out who or what is being spoken about without one name being mentioned. When they do figure it out (hopefully before the punch line comes) the laughter is almost uncontrollable.

No topic is off limits to the speechifier but a good speechifier is unlikely to ever attract a defamation suit because of the clever way that the speech is made. In the old days the speechifying also took the form of banter between two or more speechifiers. During such bantering they would threaten each other with destruction and defeat - both in the speech and also in a mock sword fight, when any one dared to challenge their greatness.

The whole event is supposed to be a clash of wills, physical strength and intellect among the speechifiers. Thus after one of the speechifiers gives a speech that poked fun at or ridiculed another speechifier, the latter would come forward to deliver a reply. He would walk straight up to the last speaker and challenge him by clashing his sword against his. They would then engage in a mock sword fight for a short while.

When that is done the "offended" speechifier would make his speech in reply usually with the aim of embarrassing the first speechifier. If he does so successfully the crowd would dissolve into laugher and clap with gusto thus indicating that as far as the crowd is concerned he had regained his honour.

The original speechifiers gave themselves names to reflect their idea of how feared they thought they should be or how fearless. So it was Hero Conqueror, Commander, Lucifer and Spitfire. Throughout the sword fight the music continued, played with increased vigour. This served to incite the rivalry further and generate more excitement in the crowd. However when one of the speechifiers moved centre stage and declared, "Stop Yuh Bow, Mr. Fiddler!", the music, dancing and moving around immediately stopped. All persons became silent in order to listen to the speech he was about to deliver. All listeners had to hear the words of the speech clearly in order to get the story and the punch line.

The delivery of the speech and the punch line are two important details in a speech band. They help to distinguish a good speech.

But speeches alone do not a great speech band make. There are other ingredients - first is the music itself. The music is indispensable to the process. In the old days music for speech band was provided mainly by the tambourine and the fiddle.

The Tobago tambourine is a slim drum-like instrument which provides accompaniment to the fiddle. The tambourine can be played to produce different sounds all of which require a player with that particular skill. First is the man who is known as the "roller". He is responsible for keeping the timing. Then there is the "boom" which provides the base sounds in the music. Next is the "cutter" which gives the music its style or "ramajay". Finally there is the man who plays the triangle, which is a small piece of iron. It helps with timing but also gives that nice ringing sound to the music.

The tambourine is made from goat skin which was soaked in water for a couple days to get it soft and "limber" (meaning pliable). This makes it easy to pull across a ring of about one yard in circumference. This ring is made of a vine known as wild cassava. The skin is then secured or stabilized on the ring and left to dry in the sun for another day or so. After this it is ready to be used.

The interesting thing about the tambourine is that it has to be given fire to make its best sounds. Thus the accompanying musicians always had a supply of dry branches available near to the stage to make a fire for heating the tambourine - if the music was to meet expectations.

The lone fiddler was a key man in the music. He was like the star of the musicians even though he did not receive as much attention as the tambourine players.

Today with fewer youngsters mastering the art of playing the fiddle and the tambourine, the musical accompaniment to the speech band is now the African drum which is easier for the young people to beat and to make. However the Tobago tambourine for the older folks had a special sweetness and attraction. They insist that its sounds were different and far superior to the drums for speech band purposes.

Another exciting part of the speech band presentation is the enjoyable way that the speechifiers dance around before they come forward to deliver their speech. You had to see the old practitioners at the game to understand. The entire presentation is introduced by the music and then one after the other each of the speechifiers would come forward to render his speech.

Before delivering his speech, he may challenge the last speaker in a mock sword fight. At the end of that sword fight he would come forward to indicate his readiness to speechify by shouting the famous command to the musicians. The command is by now internationally recognized and attributed to the island of Tobago, "*STOP YUH BOW, MR. FIDDLER!*". The music would then stop immediately and total silence would then engulf the scene as the speechifier launches into his speech. When he came to the end and hit the punch line the crowd would roar with laughter and he would shout to the musicians, "*DRAG YUH BOW, MR. FIDDLER*". The musicians then played the music once more and all the speechifiers would burst into dancing in their beautiful and infectious way. The next speaker would then come forward to make his delivery in the same manner until all the speakers have delivered two to three speeches each.

Nowadays with the absence of the fiddle, the speakers give a different command, "*STOP YUH DRUM, MR DRUMMER*" and "*BEAT YUH DRUM, MR. DRUMMER*". Of course, the old people say it is definitely not the same thing and insist that players should continue using the old command even though there is no bow and fiddle any more.

The beauty of the speech band does not end with the speeches and the music. It would not be sweet speech band if it did not come with the gaily coloured satin costumes that the speechifiers wear, and the style of the costume, too. The costume took the form of a brightly coloured satin shirt with a three quarter length pantaloon or even a skirt just as colourful as the shirt. They wanted it to shine in the sun.

Some of the well-known figures like Charlie Leith used to wear a knee-length skirt of the same satin over the pantaloon. They would decorate their costumes with all types of trinkets: small mirrors, small medals, lanyards, and military style "caggage". Most of all they would drape what was called a "swash" of the same satin cloth across their shoulder running sideways and gather it in a knot at the side of the body.

The shoes that they wore were known as "washecong" - low cut sneakers - or the "jim boots" (or is it "gym boots")? They were spray-painted in silver, gold or other Carnival colours.

Long ago, the speechifiers would also use white powder on their faces. But the main item on their face was a mask known as the "the facen". So in the old days a speechifier was only recognized by his voice, mannerisms, body language and the kind of speech he delivered.

On their heads they wore the most unusual head gear one has ever seen. It was called a "cock hat" or speech band hat. It was a boat-shaped design made out of bamboo or light wood with an opening into which one's head would fit. The maker would then decorate it with colourful kite paper, plastic and strings. Normally the player would tie a head tie on his head before putting on the cock hat.

In his hand each player would carry a short brightly painted or decorated sword, which he would wave around with panache as he danced on stage or delivered his speech. The sword was like his tool of trade. It was also used by an offended speechifier to indicate to the offender that he was challenging him on a speech already delivered.

In all this get-up those in the crowd sometimes had difficulty in recognizing the speaker unless his girth, way of speech or mannerism was familiar to them.

3. THE BAND LAUNCHING

One of the most beautiful activities to watch was the "band launching". That was usually held on Carnival Sunday night in a big yard somewhere in the village.

This was the gala event and it was when the crowning of the King of the Speech band took place. You had to be there to believe it! Almost the entire village used to turn out to watch and even dance around the area with the band. Parents did not like children attending the launching mainly because of the suggestiveness in the speeches. Some of us found ourselves there any way. And it was a beautiful night of speeches, tambourine and fiddle music and dancing by all the villagers.

The several speeches were intended to select the best speechifier and to crown him as the King of Speech band for that year. This was the moment for each speechifier to excel and win the crown. Each of them in delivering his speech and presenting himself would try to be the best in wit, humour and rhyme. If he does so, with outstanding grace, poise, bravado and panache while brandishing his sword, then he would be hard to beat. My favourite in all these categories was a gentleman known as "Mr. Jimmie Lyons". For me, he was the best - especially in poise and grace. The contest would see each speechifier challenging his opponent to come before him to be demolished in speech, like this:

> *"Appear Valantine Appear.*
> *Appear and face you maker right here.*
> *Let me destroy every grain of yuh hair."*

After the launching, the band would go to the homes of a few villagers on the Monday morning giving speeches and dancing. The villager would give them a nice tip for their entertainment. To this day, I remember one of the speeches delivered in the yard of my parents Mr. and Mrs. Moore. That day, a neighbour and friend of my mother, Mrs. Skeete, was visiting. With skilful improvisation, the speechifier declared:

> *"Stop yuh bow, Mr. Fiddler!*
> *This is the village of Bethel*
> *Where we the people does live so well*
> *But never have two people lived so sweet*
> *Like Mrs. Moore and Mrs. Skeete*
> *Drag yuh bow Mr. Fiddler!"*

The next day, Carnival Tuesday, the band formed up in the village to begin its long trek to the competition venue in Scarborough. Carnival Tuesday morning - a day usually blessed by brilliant sunshine and with excitement in the air. One of the best experiences in the world then was when the speech band came out on the road to begin its trek to the competition venue in Scarborough. The speech band has its own category in the Carnival competition. The tambourine and fiddle would strike up the music and players and the spectators alike would immediately start to dance on the street. Thus began the long march to Scarborough from Bethel – a distance of about five miles.

The players had a most dramatic way chipping on the streets to the music. I will never forget the way they walked and danced their way into town. Many of the villagers just could not leave the music and turn back so they followed them all the way into Scarborough, dancing as they went to the sweet music of the tambourine and fiddle. Of course the group had to stop along the way to heat up the tambourines and refresh themselves but no one minded that at all.

So there they were - the Bethel Pepper Ants Speech Band – all ten to fifteen players and musicians, led by the indomitable Charlie Leith. Dressed in full regalia – colourful satin costume glittering in the sun, bright red, green, blue and yellow cockhats on their head, facen or white powder on their faces and swords in hand. This band was an incredibly beautiful sight chipping on the road making their way to Scarborough with a whole group of villagers dancing behind them.

Yes, we totally enjoyed it. No Tobagonian is complete unless he has witnessed a speech band launch and the crowning of the king … or unless he has jumped behind that speech band into Scarborough! This is what makes us Tobagonian – enjoying a good Tobago speech band.

ODE TO THE TOBAGO SPEECH BAND
Deborah Moore-Miggins

"Stop yuh Bow Mr. Fiddler!
Good evening Ladies and Gentlemen all
A pleasant Good Evening I bid to you all
We thank you for answering the call
To come out to the Band Launching of the Pepper Ants Speech
Band in this hall.

The Speech Band is Tobago greatest art form
When yuh hear the "drag yuh bow, Mr. Fiddler",
It is this sunny isle with people so friendly and oh so warm
Is about seven players in a band dat used to perform
De name of the bands was as if they was the baddest champion
As though they go defeat yuh in any kind ah competition
Names like Conquistadores, Speechifiers and Pepper Ants go
beat yuh to scorn
And de players deyself did get names like Spitfire and
Commander and dey truly transform
From sweet village gentlemen to warriors …like a raging
thunderstorm.

Dey use to go all over the world to perform
Telling everybody about what de country have going on
From who making baby to who getting horn
And which politician behave badly so that's why he gone.

Carnival time they hold de band launching wid de whole village
looking on

And dey crowning the King of the Speech band from how
dey perform
Was excitement for so Carnival Sunday night from dusk till
dawn
Den on Carnival Monday dey come to yuh home so beautifully
adorn
Bedecked in dey bright satin colours that was they uniform
Wid a satin sash across and a colourful cock hat and carrying
dey sword
And with powder and mask on face they would kick up a
storm
And is speech after speech dat they used to perform.

De men playing tambrin and fiddle must be wid dem on that
Carnival morn
Dey would heat up de tambrin with fire right dey on yuh lawn
Was the sweetest music you ever hear in any manner or form
But make sure yuh yourself noh have no dutty business yuh
carrying on
Cause dey go expose yuh in speech and is gone dey gone. *Drag
yuh bow Mr. Fiddler!*

De African Dimension

Deborah Moore-Miggins

We celebrating Black History Month now in dis November
It is good that we pay tribute to the mother country Africa
For giving us plenty of African brother and sister
So that we in Tobago can all live together
So today we pay nuff respect and great honour
To all de great people who was we African ancestor
To all of them who endure the Middle Passage and come ya
Yes, it is good that someone remind us to remember

That we standing here today means we came from a brave
survivor
Who was strong enough to survive the journey to come ova
The others just could not endure the horror
Some dead from suffocation, dysentery and cholera
And others was killed off by diarrhoea
Then it have dem who decide to dive straight into the water
Rather than remain on de ship... forever?
Going to a place that could never be better
Than dey great and beloved Africa

Africa was the country that was the most advanced of all nation
It was known all over as the cradle of civilization
The African people of old excelled in all kinds of invention
They were the masters of medicine, mathematics and
navigation
They was planters and reapers and did plenty cultivation

And don't talk 'bout business and trading, Africa was a champion
Black people came to distinguish themselves with great innovation
Like Lewis Latimer who invented the light bulb and air condition
And Charles Drew he gave us the Blood Bank and blood preservation
Then Sarah Goode get several patents for creating furniture - the first black woman.

Don't talk about Breedlove and Madame Walker they make dollars by the million
for their creation of some hair care solution
Elijah McCoy made the real McCoy for vehicle lubrication
Garrett Morgan he made the gas mask to assist in fire explosion
And the traffic lights to prevent vehicle collision
Glanville Woods for telephone communication
The pressure cooker, paper and refrigeration
All came from the minds of persons who was African

But ah find we ah dis country noh really understand
De meaning of dat great African dimension
We slow to create, to invent or to produce anything of distinction
We don't want to follow the footsteps of Ellie Mannette and Spree Simon
Who created the world famous Trinbago steel pan
But we children don't even want to study for a science qualification

Instead all of them want to do arts, law and communication
And claiming that business is not the strong point of de black
man

They want a job from somebody rather than create it by their
own action
Some of them idling by the road corner getting into trouble
and altercation
Wid dey pants hanging way down below the downward
position
Instead of doing things that would bring them reward and
admiration
We women cyant walk the street in peace without molestation
Is rape, is robbery, violence and even abduction
And we too wesself we Tobago woman
We does dress in a way like if we have no appreciation
That we come from a great African tradition
And that the mark of a good woman
Is we intellect, we character and human compassion
And not we raiment or external decoration

So today when we celebrate Black History Month in this little
island
We must act as though we know about the African dimension
In we composition
And show that we full of creativity, intelligence and ambition
Dat we is a proud people with a sense of direction
And that life for us did not begin on the slave plantation
And we confident … doing great things in this land
Because we know what it means to be African.

The Caribbean Bush Bath
Deborah Moore-Miggins

Almost every Caribbean boy or girl of years gone by has lived through the experience of having a bush bath. For some the bath was for a specific purpose and for others a bush bath was routinely administered by the parent just before the start of the new school year.

A purge and a bush bath were a must-do when school children were going out to school in the new school year. The purge was mainly with senna, aloes or castor oil. The bush for the bath included black sage, toolsie, corraille better known as "papa loh loh", soursop, bayleaf - all of which were meticulously collected by the parent or grandparents days before the bath.

Some Caribbean parents believed that a bush bath was necessary to ward off evil and negative forces from their children. Other parents simply bathed their children with bush and gave them the purge mainly because it was part of a total regimen to clean them up after two months of school vacation.

It was thought that the bush would clean the skin of all the impurities that may have developed in the body from eating different things or playing in different places over the year. The bath was even intended to eradicate lice from the heads of some children.

For those children who were being bathed simply to clean them up for the new school year they were lucky to be bathed in the 'big-eye daytime', (as we used to say). The bath involved the soaking of the bush in a bucket with water for a few hours for the water to get warm. Using a bar of blue soap, the bather would bathe the child all over, making sure to "sap" or beat the bush against all areas of the body including the head.

The parent would also scrub vigorously all parts of the child's body talking to the child throughout teaching him/her how to bathe properly. They would concentrate their scrubbing on the areas where dirt accumulates, when not attended to during regular baths. The bath went on for about 10 minutes during which the water (which had by then turned totally green) was running down all areas of the body including the face, eyes, ears and mouth. If they were six children in the home all six of them would have to go through this ritual one by one. Somehow most children did not mind this type of bath even if a green bush or two was found lurking in their hair the next day.

It was a real nightmare however for those children especially teenagers whose parents gave them a bush bath to "ward off evil". This was the bath most children resented as they were bathed in the dead of night. Their bath was accompanied by a speech that went like this:

"Ah know you aint believe in dese tings but it have evil all around. People go envy yuh especially now that you pass for high school. So you does have to protect yuhself. Yuh cyant take chances. So we go give you a bath with some bush and tings. Dis aint mean nutten not no obeah business. Is just that you have to protect yourself.

While this speech was being delivered the parent or grandparent led the child to the stand pipe in the back yard next where the bucket with the water and bush stood. This water was usually mixed with lavender, lime, black disinfectant and indigo blue, (used for washing clothes). All this was thought to be effective in cutting evil, envy, hatred and 'bad mind').

In no time the child's clothes were off and he was being bathed with the horrible smelling mixture and the blue soap. All his hair, ears, mouth and eyes were caught up with this lavender, blue soap and blue, bush mixture. If the case was extreme, a bible verse would be repeated during the bath. At the end of it the child is told not to wash the mixture off his skin.

One such "bath victim" (now a big man) recounted to friends the experience, which he certainly did not enjoy, of being bathed with this concoction in the middle of the night. His friends went into stitches of laughter as they heard of the occasion when he was about 12 years old. His mother and her boyfriend virtually held him down and put a bush bath on him – "sapping" him from head to toe with the bush and foul-smelling liquid. The final nail in the coffin was when they told him not to "wash it off."

He has been angry for years about the incident. He said that he was glad that it occurred in the middle of the night when he thought no one could have seen but he was wrong because the next day, an inquisitive cousin who lived upstairs said to him:

"*They bathe yuh wid bush last night?*"

He replied, with embarrassment, "*No.*"

She said, "*Yes! I smelled the ting from up here and when I look out ah see them bathing you.*"

He had to mumble an answer and disappear quickly from the scene but that was not the end of his embarrassment. The worst part was that the next day his white school shirt collar turned blue causing the children at school to look at him strangely. More than that, when he began to perspire, the children could not contain their laughter at the sight of blue perspiration running down his face!

To this day, he thanks God that the children did not start to call him "Blue Sweat"!

$\mathscr{T}$helma Perkins

THELMA PERKINS was born in Birmingham UK during the 2nd world war, to a Jewish mother & Trinidadian father (Ernest Mckenzie-Mavinga).

Trained as a nurse, she later moved into teaching after studying for a Bachelor of Education degree. 1994 saw the publication of "In Search of Mr McKenzie" in *The Women's Press,* which she co-wrote with her sister. It was while researching for this book that she and her sister discovered their Trinidadian family. This was the catalyst for her decision make her home with her husband on the island of Tobago when they retired.

Other publications include a story for children "Wishing on a Wooden Spoon", *Mantra Publishing and several short* stories included in anthologies. Her first novel "Roundabouts", *Mango publishing,* is set in London.

She continues to write for both children and adults

GOING HOME
Thelma Perkins

The day she was due to fly to Jamaica, Mavis overslept. She had been up until the early hours of the morning, packing her over-sized suitcase and worrying about how her children and grandchildren would manage while she was away. After forty years she was going back home. But it looked as if she was going to miss the flight.

Mavis Elizabeth Gloria Rankin arrived in South East London on the 8th of October 1959. Two days after her twentieth birthday. She had left her two-year old son Gary behind, with her parents in Jamaica. Mavis had saved half her wages for a year until she had sufficient money to purchase a single air ticket to join Gary's father, Godfrey, in London.

Her Auntie Icylyn and her husband Vernon, with whom she was to stay, met her at the airport. Auntie Icylyn talked non-stop throughout the journey to the tall, flat fronted, three-storey house on Brockley Road, Lewisham. Mavis, sat on the back seat of the grey Ford Zephyr car, her eyes wide as saucers watching rows of terraced houses pass by. Every time Uncle Vernon swung the car around a corner, Mavis slid from one side of the car to the other on the long, smooth, pale blue, imitation leather seat.

Her excitement at finally achieving her first real goal in life was tempered somewhat by the realisation that there didn't appear to be any trees in London and that all the houses were either grey or white with black front doors. Her eyes nearly popped out of her head when she saw a block of flats. "Yu mean to say Auntie, dat people have to walk up hundreds of stairs and along dem verandas to get to dem home and dat famblies does live behind each of dem doors?"

"Yes, girl. And remember now that you is in England you have to talk proper, same as you did in school. English people don't understand that country talk. You hear me?"

"Yes Auntie, me hear you. Auntie have you seen Godfrey?'

"Yes me have, an' him will come round to see you at the weekend. But let me tell you now Miss Mavis Rankin, you have come here to do the nurse training not to make no more babies with Godfrey Brown."

"Yes Auntie, no Auntie."

Mavis grabbed hold of the padded door moulding as the car swung in a wide arc around a corner.

Icylyn re-embarked on her conversation to tell Mavis about the job she had managed to secure for her in a local laundry until she could get herself enrolled in a nursing training course.

The house in Brockley with its tiny front garden and thick net curtains became home to Mavis for five years. She shared a double bed and a large heavy oak wardrobe, in a small room, on the first floor with her cousin Diana. Auntie Icylyn and Uncle Vernon's room was on the ground floor behind the front room. It had French windows that opened on to a long strip of hard, bare grey-brown earth that served for a garden. A narrow passage led from the front door past these two rooms to the kitchen and a lean-to bathroom, used only by family members. The rest of the occupants of the house, predominantly men, made weekly journeys to the public facilities in Laurie Grove, New Cross for a bath. All the doors including the one to the front sitting room were kept locked.

Mavis was awakened several times each morning between four and six o'clock, when she got up, by the sound of a key being turned in a lock.

There were five rooms on the upper two floors of the house. Mavis and Diana shared one. The remaining four were occupied by other recent arrivals from the Caribbean who worked all manner of shifts. They entered and left the house at various times of the day and night. The lodgers shared a cooker and a sink housed in a small recess on the first floor landing next to the room in which Mavis slept. The smell of the food combined with paraffin fumes permeated every room assailing Mavis's nostrils when she entered the house, a smell that even pervaded her clothes.

Mavis had arrived in London on a Friday. The following Monday she commenced work in the laundry of Hither Green hospital. Her job was to sort the linen – bloody, urine-soaked, faeces-stained sheets, towels, nappies and gowns. Everyone who worked in the laundry, except for the supervisors was either Irish or from the Caribbean. All with hopes and dreams of making sufficient money in the next three to five years before returning home. She worked from eight in the morning until six o'clock. The work was heavy and tiring, the laundry hot and noisy and everyone shouted at each other in order to make themselves heard.

During her first winter in England, Mavis was grateful for the steamy, hot atmosphere of the laundry particularly if she had been unable to catch a bus in Lewisham and, fearful of being late, had walked up Davenport Road, bundled in her thick coat, scarf, gloves and winter boots to arrive panting from the exertion, though shivering from the cold, to clock on.

On Sundays she went to church with her aunt and uncle accompanied by her cousin Diana and Godfrey, who always came back with them to the house for dinner. Initially they attended the local parish church. However, Auntie Icylyn, a recent convert to Christianity, who claimed Jesus to be her one true friend and who had consequently given up smoking thirty cigarettes a day, declared that the vicar of the church was a cold man with hands like a wet fish, eyes that were not truthful and also that he did not make her or her family feel welcome in *his* church, found a small gathering of similarly minded immigrants who worshipped in a local mission hall and subsequently shepherded them all there.

Unfortunately Mavis wasn't accepted for training as a state registered nurse. She was told to apply to the nursing school again to train as an enrolled nurse, (more practical than theoretical) which she did. The letter advising her that the class for September '60 was oversubscribed arrived one week later. She decided to apply again the following year. Meanwhile she and Godfrey began saving through a *'pardner' scheme, their aim being to buy their own home and get married. Somehow Mavis overlooked the application date for 1961 and New Year 1962 found her wrapped in Godfrey's arms, on his bed, in his small room, elsewhere in Brockley.

Mavis continued to work in the laundry. Three years after her arrival in London Auntie Icylyn helped to arrange her wedding to Godfrey. Following their marriage in Lewisham registry office she allowed the couple to rent the larger of the two attic rooms in the house for three pounds and ten shillings a week. They shared a toilet and the cooker on the landing with the other tenants. However her aunt allowed her to use the ground floor bathroom with its noisy gas geyser once a week, because she was family. Otherwise she made do with a 'strip' wash in the attic room using hot water heated in a kettle on top of one of the two paraffin heaters they used to keep the cold at bay.

The room with its sloping ceiling and built-in cupboard appeared large. However it was soon filled with Mavis and Godfrey's possessions leaving little space to move around the double bed, Godfrey's radiogram and the small drop-leaf dining table. Mavis bought a candlewick bedspread from Pecry's in Deptford. She paid for it in weekly instalments of two shillings and sixpence. She also managed to acquire bed linen, towels and a set of enamel saucepans in the same manner.

This room was where Mavis spent her first Christmas as Mrs Brown. Her present to Godfrey was two Rael Brook shirts, purchased from the Indian salesman who called every Saturday afternoon with a large battered brown suitcase that contained an assortment of clothing and small household goods. He too, collected payments in weekly instalments. Godfrey gave Mavis a shiny green, quilted, satin housecoat.

On Boxing Day, 1963 it began to snow. It snowed for four days. By the end of the week almost all of England was at a standstill, covered in a blanket of white.

Mavis who was four months pregnant walked to and from work every day. It was only the thought of the warmth of the laundry that sustained her as she slipped and slid and struggled up one hill and down another on her journey.

She soon lost her enchantment with snow!

Then a freezing frost set in that locked the country into a three-month state of paralysis. Godfrey, who worked as a carpenter on the building sites, was laid off work – a big disappointment to both of them, because although Godfrey signed on as unemployed there was insufficient money to enable them to continue playing two 'pardners' and also send money home to Mavis' parents for the care of Gary.

Godfrey was to remain out of work until the end of March.

Their second son, David, was born in May. Six weeks after his birth Mavis returned to work. Auntie Icylyn looked after the baby during the day along with three other children. On Saturdays Mavis shopped, cleaned and visited the launderette, the baby's pram piled high with the little family's washing. Before she went to bed on Saturday night Mavis cut up and seasoned a chicken and put the red peas to soak for the following day's dinner. She always woke on Sunday with the intention of accompanying Godfrey and her auntie's family to church. However, faced with a mountain of ironing, dinner to complete and numerous other tasks she would send Godfrey off promising to join them the following week.

Monday morning came too soon for Mavis Brown.

David was five months old when Mavis realised that she was once again pregnant. Exhausted after a day in the laundry and later climbing up two flights of stairs with the baby screaming to be fed in one arm and a bag of groceries on the other. She began to cry. She wept as she prepared a bottle for her howling son. She wept as she sat on the edge of the pink covered bed and fed him his Milo. She wept for the baby son she had left behind in Jamaica and had promised to send for; for the career that would once again have to be deferred and the postponement of the purchase of a house of their own because once again she would have to stop work. This time she probably would not get maternity allowance.

Shortly after the birth of another son Anthony, and just as Mavis was preparing to return to work, her aunt called her into the kitchen. She took the baby from Mavis, who remained on her feet to follow fourteen-month-old David as he toddled around the kitchen and opened cupboard doors, reached for handles or attempted to explore the waste bin.

Auntie Icylyn squashed the tiny baby to her large breasts and rocked him fiercely as she told the stunned Mavis that she and Godfrey would have to find somewhere else to live. Although Mavis agreed that the room was far from big enough for her family she wondered how Icylyn proposed to fit her own three teenaged boys that were due from Jamaica in six weeks' time, into it.

"What me going to do?" Mavis asked her friend Cynthia Cameron, who unlike Mavis, had managed to qualify as an enrolled nurse and was working on the geriatric wards of the hospital. Cynthia not only gave her the address of a vacant three-roomed ground floor flat but also suggested that she apply to work three or four nights a week, as an auxiliary nurse at the same hospital where she worked in the laundry.

"You will make more money doing nights and you won't have to pay nobody to mind the children during the day 'cos you will be at home. Godfrey will be there at night when you is working."

The Brown family moved into the flat in nearby Forest Hill. The landlord was a Jamaican who owned several properties in southeast London, all painted in the same colours of pale blue and cream.

Mavis began to work nights. She worked Tuesday through to Friday. On Saturday morning she left the hospital and walked down to Lewisham market, where she did her shopping before, laden with heavy bags she caught a bus home.

She didn't sleep on Saturdays. Not that she really slept on Wednesday, Thursday or Friday morning either. Her young sons were past the age of sleeping long hours and even though they remained in their cots with each other for company and biscuits, bottles and toys to play with she was ever conscious of them as they babbled to each other, rattled the cot rails, bounced up and down or grizzled for attention. She drifted in and out of sleep for three to four hours before she rose to change and feed them and prepare the evening meal. By six o'clock on Saturday evening a frazzled and weary Mavis could scarcely stand as she went automatically through the routine preparations for Sunday.

Every Sunday morning dressed in a suit and tie, Godfrey went to church. He continued to attend church throughout their married life. When the children were old enough he insisted that they accompany him. Even after they finally managed to purchase a home of their own in Catford, had sent for Gary and Mavis had given birth to two more babies, both girls, Godfrey did not give up going to church. The more Godfrey became involved in his church the less paid work he did. Until finally he stopped work altogether declaring that he was doing God's work and He would provide.

Mavis worked four nights a week for twenty years.

She lifted elderly people in and out of bed, changed wet or soiled bed linen and fed drinks to patients who either gulped them gratefully or who spat the liquid out into her face. She was verbally abused by those who refused to be administered to by a black person, ordered around by senior staff who had little or no respect for her, pinched, poked and, on occasions, hit by cantankerous or confused patients and groped by lecherous old men who grinned while cackling at her disgusted expression as she removed their faeces- engrained fingers from her breast or bottom.

Mavis had five children and one grandson when, to her surprise, she was informed by her doctor that the reason for her tiredness was because she was pregnant. She was astounded. Godfrey had just returned to Jamaica where he now lived permanently preaching and ministering to a small rural congregation. The only reason he was able to spend a month with Mavis in London was because she had paid his fare.

Sonia was born during a thunderstorm one September night. She weighed just over nine pounds. Mavis, who was in labour for fifteen hours, was exhausted. But returned to work nights when the baby was three months old. Her eldest daughter cared for the baby until a weary Mavis returned home in the morning.

"Who else going to finish paying the mortgage?" she said to Cynthia.

The only concession Mavis made was to cut down her working hours to three nights a week. She worked for another fifteen years. In that time she struggled to complete the mortgage repayments on her home. She paid for Godfrey to make periodical visits from Jamaica and she also paid the exorbitant telephone bills he somehow managed to run up.

Mavis repeatedly promised herself that she was going to return home to see her mother before she died. But somehow each time she had acquired enough for her 'plane ticket and was saving for pocket money, a financial crisis arose. She would then secure a loan to tide her over. There were days when Mavis thought that she would never ever succeed in owning her home outright as the loans were usually against the property.

"You know, Cameron," she told her friend Cynthia one morning shortly before her fifty-ninth birthday as they walked home together after a particularly stressful and heavy night on the wards, "some days I feel so tired even my heart has trouble beating."

"When you last have a holiday, Brown?"

"Oh me did have two weeks in July when me daughter had her second baby."

"And before that?"

"A week at Easter when me grandson came to stay."

"When you last have a good sleep, Brown?"

"You know, Cameron, me can't remember. There is always someone in the house, daytime, night time an weekends. If the boys not there playing music, then Sonia have her friends in or I am looking after one of the grand pickney."

"Is time you took yourself off to Jamaica for at least six weeks, girl."

"I know. But me going soon. Me going to spend me sixtieth birthday there. Is forty years since me last put eyes on me mother an me have to go before she die. Me have to."

The drive to the airport reminded Mavis of her first car ride in England. Gary's silver BMW screeched around corners at breakneck speed and hurtled along the motorway at almost a hundred miles an hour. He manoeuvred the car in and out of lanes while Mavis clutched the door and silently thanked the inventor of seat belts for ensuring that she wasn't thrown forwards, sideways or backwards out of the car. Gary's girlfriend and his son Marlon rode with them. The remainder of the family followed behind in a further three cars.

Mavis felt a wave of nausea sweep over her as the car entered the tunnel approaching Heathrow. The echo of her pounding heartbeat resounded in her ears. Her chest felt tight.

At the airport, one of the children found a trolley while the drivers of the cars went to park. Mavis and the remainder of her family headed for the check in desk.

She needed a drink of water but there wasn't time. The collective panic threatened to overwhelm her as they hustled her towards the entrance of the departure lounge.

"You okay mum?"

Perspiration oozed from her forehead, her armpits, and her thighs. She could feel rivulets running down her back as she struggled to keep up.

"You sure you will be okay?"

A band of iron around her chest was threatening to stop her breathing; her mouth opened and closed; a grey mist was descending in front of her.

"Come on Mum, don't stop there, they have given out a last call for you."

"Can you manage on your own?"

"Phew, you...forget...that...me...have...flown...before? I will be fine when me get on the plane and sit down...wheee."

Their kisses and hugs were brief. Cries of 'goodbye', 'Have a safe journey', 'Enjoy yourself and we love you', followed her when she passed through the security checks, and faded into the general melee as she retrieved her handbag and a larger bag from the conveyor belt.

People pushed past her almost knocking her over.

If only she could stop and draw breath, but she was late already and had to find the gate, get to the gate and board the plane first.

"Excuse me, I have to catch this flight. It's going from this gate. Where is it? Can you tell me where to go?"

"Which way? Oh that way. T'ank you."

Hurry up Mavis girl, you can't miss this 'plane. You going home, girl, come on now. You be fine when you on the plane.

Breath coming in ragged gasps.

Bag bumping against thigh, dragging down on the floor.

Iron band squeezing tighter.

Pick up your bag! Walk fast! Down here! Along here on the moving belt! Quick, quick!

Thighs rubbing slickly.

Bags slipping through sweaty palms.

Tongue sticking to dry roof of mouth.

Mavis is the only passenger in the final boarding area.

"In here. See that desk down there, where that lady with the red and blue scarf is waving to you?"

I'm coming, oh Jesus God wait, don't go without me.

Head pushed forward.

Breath pumping out.

Heart pounding.

Please, please.

"Are you Mavis Brown?"

"Give me your bag. Come on, dear, we are just about to close the doors."

Lift up leaden feet one by one.

Clutch tightly to thin bony arm.

Breathe slow and deep, slow and deep.

The iron band is still there.

Tighter, tighter.

"Here sit here, fasten your belt, like this; let me do it."

"I need a drink."

Tongue flicks over parched lips.

Beads of sweat on upper lip.

Hands flutter up and down.

The plane shudders; its engines roar and send vibrations through the body of the plane, through Mavis Brown whose own body shudders in anticipation.

It glides forward on smooth wheels a huge bird that lifts and rises, nose upward towards blue skies.

Simultaneously, the iron band releases its grip. There is a pain beneath her chin now and along her jaw.

"Are you all right, dear?"

The woman seated next to her looks concerned, leans forward to look into her face.

"Yes, me is good, jus the rushin to get on de plane, me nearly miss it you know."

Mavis smiles.

"First time you have flown, is it?"

The woman relaxes and sits back.

"No, no, me did come here on a BOAC plane forty years ago when me did firs' come here."

The pain in her chest seemed to have eased although the ache in her jaw was just as intense. She sipped slowly at the water the flight attendant had brought to her once the plane was airborne.

"I did save for my fare long time 'cos I didn't want to come on a ship," she added proudly.

Her neighbour appeared to have lost interest, she was now deeply engrossed in the duty free magazine.

"Long-time," Mavis mused, "yes 'tis long time me save, long time me promise I goin home, long time since me see me mumma and pappa. An now is time but I is so tired, I gwan sleep for a week."

Closing her eyes she tried to recall the Jamaica she left as a young girl. Godfrey had told her of the changes each time he returned to London to visit.

"You won't recognize Norman Manley Airport. It not called Palisades anymore, an' old city Kingston is all slum an' bruk down buildings. All the businesses move to tall buildings in New Kingston. Everywhere is fences an' gates an' security guards. They have a new highway that goes from Kingston all the way to Maypen. We have to pay a toll to get on but it worth it; now we get to Maypen quick, quick."

She thought about the house in Mandeville that he boasted of, built with money she had sent to him. Four bedrooms and three bathrooms, a wraparound balcony and burglar bars to keep the bad men out. She was looking forward to sitting out on the balcony enjoying the warmth and the breeze and meeting some of her old friends who had retired and returned.

"We even have a returnees club," he told her proudly.

"How are you feeling now, dear?"

Startled, she gasped when the cabin attendant touched her arm.

"Me good, me is good, t'ank you, t'ank-you."

"Good, good. Just press this button here if you need anything."

Mavis drifted into sleep, her mind still focussed on the sun and the breeze. Although her jaw and chin still ached the chest pains had subsided. "I just tired," she told herself. "Is like Cameron said, I need a long rest. Forty years I been working hard, hard, now me is almos sixty, time to rest, relax, tha's wha' me gwan do, relax, jus' relax."

The plane flew on up and out over the Atlantic Ocean, high above the clouds beneath blue skies. "We have perfect flying conditions today, ladies and gentlemen, so we will probably arrive at Norman Manley Airport a little earlier than scheduled. The weather forecast for Jamaica is good; sit back, relax and enjoy the flight."

Two hours out of Jamaica she awoke suddenly, the pain in her chest jolting her upright. She clutched at the pain, beads of perspiration appeared on her forehead.

"Please, please, I need…"

Her voice trails off as she is consumed with the pain. Her elbow jerks involuntarily and catches her neighbour's arm.

"Is something wrong?" she asked.

Mavis gasps, opens her eyes, her mouth, unclenches her fingers.

The pain is so intense she cannot answer. Inside her chest a fist expands in an explosion of pain. Aagh!

Someone is calling, "Help! This lady needs help."

Hands pull at her belt.

"Is there a doctor on board?"

"I'm goin home, I'm goin home. Let me sleep, I jus' tired."

They were trying to pull something over her face, calling her, pushing at her chest, asking her questions.

The 'plane flew low over the Caribbean. The iron band tightened, the fist poised. Draws back. And punches again.

Mavis closed her eyes and flew home.

Who yu Daddy?
Thelma Perkins

Who yu daddy?
Mi no know.
Who yu daddy?
Mi mammy neva tell mi.
Who yu daddy?
Mista why yu wanna know
Who mi daddy?

Who yu fava?
Where yu get yu big feet?
An yu hans so long?
Yu neva aks where yu get dem big eyes?
An yu shape head?
I bet yu is a real smart bwoy.

Mista is mi auntie who say,
I fava mi fadda,
Den mi granny she say
Hush di bwoy lissening
And mi granny tell mi
I fava me mammy.

Who yu granny?
Mi mammy's mammy.
Where yu daddy's mammy?
Mista mi no know.
Yu mean yu neva aks yu mammy
Who yu daddy?
Yu neva aks yu granny bout yu udder granny?
Yu real sure yu no know who ya daddy?
No mista dem neva tell mi.
Well bwoy
I is your daddy.
Mi a come an mi a go.

Hey mista
Is wha mi mammy say.
He a come
An he a go.

EMBRACING THE PEACE

By Dianne Chapman

I LOOKED AROUND ME; I BEHELD, I SAW BEAUTY, VAST BEAUTY.
FOR ONE TO DECLARE THERE IS NO GOD ONE MUST BE MAD.
THE OCEAN BREEZE BLEW SOFTLY UPON ME, LIKE LIPS OF LOVE
PLANTING KISSES UPON THE LIPS OF A LOVER.

MY EARS LISTENED ATTENTIVELY TO THE MUSIC SUNG ON
THE SEAGULLS' BEAK, AS.....
I BREATHE IN EMBRACING THE PEACE THAT SURROUNDED,
HAPPY TO BE ALIVE, AS I CRUSHED SAND BETWEEN MY TOES,
MY EXPRESSION WAS ONE OF JOY;

I KNEW I WAS SMILING FOR I COULD FEEL THE SIDES OF MY
LIPS RISE WITH PLEASURE.
I WAS ALIVE AND GIVEN THE OPPORTUNITY TO EMBRACE
THE PEACE.

THE WAVES BROKE IN RHYTHMIC MOTION ALMOST
SYNCHRONIZED,
 AS THEY DANCED TO THE MUSIC OF THEIR OWN TUNE.
THE SEAGULLS FLEW SO LOW YOU COULD ALMOST TOUCH
THEM.

HOW CAN YOU DECLARE THAT THERE IS NO GOD?
ONLY THOSE WHO HAVE NOT TAKEN THE TIME TO LOOK
AROUND,
TO BEHOLD THE BEAUTY THAT SURROUNDS US, DECLARE
SUCH FOLLY.

YOU MUST LEARN, YOU NEED TO LEARN TO LOOK AROUND,
BEHOLD THE BEAUTY THAT SURROUNDS YOU
AND LEARN TO EMBRACE THE PEACE.

THE TWO SIDES OF TIME
By Dianne Chapman

THE TWO SIDES OF TIME, CAME TO THE MIND,
THE LEFT AND THE RIGHT, THE BLIND AND THE
SIGHTED,
THE DEAF, THOSE WHO HEAR; THE BURDENS
YOU BEAR,
WHEN THE TWO SIDES OF TIME UNRAVEL, YOU
FEAR.

LIFE AND DEATH, JOY AND SORROW,
PAIN AND HEALTH, FACE TOMORROW;
HOPE AND DESPAIR, THEY HAVE NO FEAR,
WANT YOU TO CARE WHEN THEY APPEAR.

RIGHT AND WRONG, DESPERATE SONG,
SHORT OR LONG, UNLIMITED BOUND,
TALL OR SHORT, A MYSTERY THOUGHT,
WHEN THE TWO SIDES OF TIME COME TO THE
MIND.

WIDE AND NARROW, BRIGHTER TOMORROW,
UP AND DOWN, AROUND AND AROUND,
NIGHT AND DAY, ONE DAY WILL PASS AWAY,
WHEN THE TWO SIDES OF TIME,
WILL BE AS ONE DAY.

HEAVEN AND EARTH, GIVING NEW BIRTH,
IN AND OUT TELL IT ALL ABOUT,
VICTORY SOUGHT, NO PURPOSE ABORT,
WHEN THE TWO SIDES OF TIME COME TO THE
MIND.

ALPHA AND OMEGA, FIRST AND THE LAST,
BEGINNING AND END AS YOUR WORD COMES
TO PASS,
WHEN YOUR VOICE ECHOES THROUGH TIME,
TO DECLARE YOU SUBLIME,
NIGHT TURNS TO DAY AND DAY INTO NIGHT,
KNOWING IN THEE IT WILL BE ALL RIGHT,
WHEN THE TWO SIDES OF TIME COME TO THE
MIND.

Reginald O. Phillips

Reginald O. Phillips (R.O.P.) is a farmer domiciled at Shirvan Road, Buccoo, in the island of Tobago.

He has already published two books: A LITERARY EXCURSION and POETIC POTPOURI and will publish his first novel before December, 2014.

R.O.P. is husband of Elizabeth Jerry-Phillips and father of Achi-Kemba Phillips, Zola Phillips, Dr Pushpa Phillips- Fortuchang, and Anson Roy.

MAMMA MI DEAR

(Reginald O. Phillips)

I hold my mother's memory
Most dearly to my heart.
There are things I really
treasure
But Mom stands quite apart.
So speak ill of my family
Whether guessing or for sure
But when you speak ill of my
mom
Is fight you looking for.

My father worked quite
yeomanly
He raised us like he should
He made provision like a man
Head of the home he stood.
Tell me my father was a scamp
Stole things from shop and store
But if you speak ill of my mom
Is fight you looking for.

My brothers and my cousins all
Are kind and loving too.
They epitomize a family
That's really good to you
Tell me they're rascals, thieves
and bums

Say this and even more
But when you gossip 'bout my
mom
Is fight you looking for

My teachers and my friends at
school
Helped me through thick and
thin
I owe so much to all of them
For what they've always been.
Yet I'll forgive you if you say
Their help to me was poor
But if you whisper 'bout my
mom
Is fight you looking for.

In my church congregation
We take a solemn vow
To love our fellow Christians
Much as time will allow
I won't mind if you speak of
them
As hypocrites galore
But if you criticize my mom
Is fight you looking for.

MEMORIES
The Passing of A.N.R.
By Reginald O. Phillips

When I think of him, I picture him playing childhood games at school, reciting poems and tables, singing lustily the Colonial songs uplifting the king and the British Empire.

When I think of him, I see in my mind's eye a country student dressed the part, spick and span, on way to school in town, behaving in manner demanded by parents of the day.........Obedient, respectful, well mannered, and kind.

When I think of him, I try to imagine a youngster from Castara, from Bishop's, leaving Tobago for the Empire city of London, taking the home training, the school pledges, the neighbourhood advice and general village upbringing, taking all of this burden of preparation to a distant land where the elitism, the sophistication of our Colonial masters would form the super structure on this tribal foundation.

I remember him coming home full of qualifications on paper and knowledge in mind, expecting the old Tobago to welcome its long lost son. I remember this brilliant graduate of Economics and Political Science being humbled on the altar of politics by one A.P.T. James who could hardly spell the word university, who never knew where Bishop's High School was located. I remember him bouncing back from that defeat and rising dramatically in political prestige to the point of openly challenging the might of the Doc and placing Tobago snugly in his pocket, so to speak. I relive the memory of Tobago East being dubbed D.A.C. City with Elvira Job, Byron and Bovell fighting like the three musketeers to enhance and preserve the dignity of the man.

I can still hear the echo of that Tobago voice in the hallowed halls of Parliament presenting an unchallengeable motion for Self- Government for his homeland.

I recall the obstinacy of a President standing in defiance of those who made him President, pointing out to his principals the error of their ways, quoting streams into rivers and rivers into seas as justification for his stance.

Greater mortals stood in awe as this Castara kid convinced the United Nations of the wisdom of creating and establishing an International Court of Justice to hound and punish even criminals with no home base.

I still hear the reverberating order of the Commander- in-chief instructing his soldiers to disregard his personal safety and ATTACK WITH FULL FORCE.

This is the man I remember, Arthur Napoleon Raymond Robinson

This is the Statesman the world has buried.

UP PULTNEY HILL
(The burning of the Tobago Farm School)
By Reginald O. Phillips

1. Your majesty was never in a doubt
    Amidst the verdant green serenely you stood out
    Commanding such a panoramic view
    Artists of every type were drawn to you.

2. Shelter you offered both to man and beast
    Seafarers marked you North, South, West, and
    East
    Rock solid there you stood atop that hill
    Natural disasters left you standing still.

3. Massa lived within your solid walls
    Priests and students paced your hallowed halls
    Teaching, learning, also meditating
    A site picturesque and tantalizing.

4. Plans were in train, we're told, to use you well
    Secretive plans so far no one can tell
    It's obvious for planners all to see
    How useful and convenient you could be.

5. Out of the blue you stand no more aloof
    Flames engulfing grounds and walls and roof
    Obliterating history and beauty
    You will remain enshrined in memory.

Carron Rivers

CARRON RIVERS was born on the 2nd of January 1960 to Mr. and Mrs. Thomas Rivers of Crooks River, Scarborough, Tobago.

She attended St. Joseph's Convent, Tobago and Harmon School of S.D.A and entered nursing in 1982. She was trained at the School of Nursing, tertiary level, the Advance School of Nursing and the School of Midwifery, at the University of the West Indies.

She is now a District Health Visitor with 32 years' nursing experience and has other certificates to her name.

Carron is a mother of two beautiful children – Mmyeka and Krystofau and also mother to her deceased sister's children – Genniq and Shenniq. She is an adopted mother and aunt to many.

Her hobbies are writing poems, listening to inspirational music, watching cartoons and soul moving movies, chatting with and counseling youngsters.

REPAIR
(Carron Rivers)

Hello! You there
Don't just stare
Repair!
Repair the damage that you have done to my brain
When you popped drugs and now leave me insane
Repair the absence of mind that you claimed
When you left me out in the rain
Repair the neglected time
Time and time again
When you abandoned me
All for the sake of a day's gain
And with an aim
To leave me behind
A shadow of your pain

Repair the abuse from four to eighteen
When you languished on my body for pleasure and fame
And selfishly forgot that I was and I'm still your child
With your name. Yes! Your name.
A name to be repaired.
A name to be renamed.
So, repair me, Daddy
Repair me, Mummy
Don't just stare
Repair!

GOSPEL IN THE GHETTO

(Carron Rivers)

Gospel in the ghetto
The guns ring out each day
Gospel in the ghetto
A young man cries 'no pay'
Gospel in the ghetto
Licks and blows and cuss
J'Ouvert
Gospel in the ghetto
A mother and her hungry
child pray and pray and pray

Ghetto life respects no man
Ghetto life no gift to man
The young are starved. The
old to blame
Ghetto life, a life of pain
A mother and her hungry
child pray and pray and pray
Gospel in the ghetto
Still a way of life today

Gospel in the ghetto
I-man singing alleluia and
hugging guns
Gospel in the ghetto
Gang man praying to win
the warfare in town
Gospel in the ghetto

Drug man dodging bullets
with mammy prayers
Gospel in the ghetto
Ras man smoking up the
place with incense and
covering hairs

Ghetto life, a sinful life
Who is to judge? What is
good life?
Ghetto life a struggling life
The poor, the hungry, some
kill to feed
Ghetto life, a life so real
A mother and her hungry
child pray and pray and pray
Another way of life for them,
some day, one day

Gospel in the ghetto
Criminals correcting their
children and asking the
master to protect them from
criminals
Gospel in the ghetto
Youth men protecting their
lives with knives in book

bags and, dope in school
yards
Gospel in the ghetto

All the streets celebrate
Christmas, Eid, Divali, and
Easter
Gospel in the ghetto

A mother and her hungry
child receive a saviour
Gospel in the ghetto
A new mother and her
hungry child pray for a
deliverer
Gospel in the ghetto
Forever and ever......

CHAOS
(Carron Rivers)

When square pegs *masculate in round holes
Chaos, chaos.
And wrong is right and good no longer the goal
Chaos, chaos
When pure hate is now the norm at day break
And a witness to crime is now dead bait
Chaos, absolute chaos.
When teenage pregnancy is now more than a way of life
Chaos, chaos
And gangsters and murderers are now youngsters with
knives
Chaos, chaos
When a supposedly loved one resorts to rape, murder and
guile and
Child abuse and molestation are now more common than a
housefly
Chaos, absolute chaos.
When bandits no longer fear police nor guns
Chaos, chaos
And boast of the number of dead men's ghosts that they tote
around
Chaos, chaos
When guns are now at a peak and bodies continue to colour
the street
Chaos, absolute chaos
When oil leaks out because sabotage creeps in
Chaos, chaos

And the rise in crime just keeps escalating
Chaos, chaos
When politicians hope for a brighter day but sit and ridicule
each other day after day
Chaos, absolute chaos
When health care no longer relaxes the heart
Chaos, chaos
And attitudes and attributes are now so far apart
Chaos, chaos
When Adam and Adam say I do and, Jenny and Jackie
decide on it too
Chaos, absolute chaos.

*masculate: to make strong

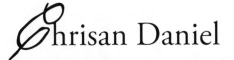hrisan Daniel

CHRISAN DANIEL was born in Laventille, Trinidad to proud parents both of whom are Tobagonians. While Chrisan was growing up in Trinidad, her mother always encouraged her love for storytelling and reading by telling her stories of growing up in Tobago. She regaled her with anecdotes of Tobago's folkloric history as well as the village stories about Mason Hall.

At the age of ten (10) Chrisan's mother moved the family to Tobago where she easily adapted to the Tobago life, so real and enlightening were the stories her mother had told her of her life in Tobago.

Chrisan's love for the Tobago culture grew tremendously when she began to dream and write stories and poems about her experiences of Tobago. Her readers relate easily to her writings and they are able to grow personally from her experiences and their own.

She currently resides in Carnbee, Tobago with her husband and is a proud mother of six (6) children. She enjoys telling them stories the way her mother did when she was a child. She also attends the University of the Southern Caribbean pursuing her BSc degree in Social Work and intends shortly to pursue a second degree in West Indian History.

What Happened to Hyacinth?
By Chrisan Daniel

I was awakened out of a deep sleep by the thudding noise made by the breadfruit tree that was situated at the back of the yard of my aunt's house. I lay silent trying to gather my thoughts. I realized I had once again wet the bedding that was my personal property in my humble space beneath the claw-footed mahogany table under which I had been sleeping for the past two years. The table was varnished in a deep dark brown colour with a cream lace cloth hanging down about six inches from the top.

I quietly glanced across with my heavily sleep-filled eyes trying to locate my sister in the darkness of the room to see if she had awakened from her sleep as well. She did not even stir as she lay tightly wrapped up in her pink peacock sheet that she brought from our home when our mother had passed away suddenly and without any warning. It had affected us very deeply. Her sister, Aunty Gertie, was very close to her so she took the responsibility of raising us two. "Cock a doodle do!" I had jumped just a little when I heard the harrowing sound of the yard cock beckoning the day and knew that the whole household would become alive in a short while.

I sucked my teeth after I had done my usual body stretching as though to throw off the sleepiness until another time. I looked up into my private table-top ceiling, closed my eyes and said a prayer. I jumped when I felt my body being shaken by my sister Hyacinth, telling me that it was time to get up.

I was a bit startled because I had drifted back into sleep, while I was saying my morning prayer. I did a quick stretch, crawled out from beneath the table and pulled out my bedding to take outside to get its usual sunning. "Hurry up girl," Hyacinth said to me as she started to retie her green and white polka dot head tie that had become loose during her time sleeping. I quickly gathered up in my bedding and carried it outside, putting it on the fencing on the right side of the house.

The house which stood on four concrete posts contained one bedroom and a living room and was parted off with a door to the only bedroom that our aunt occupied. The house stood facing west with each room containing two windows and a door each. I went beneath the house to collect my sweet broom that I had made for myself to do my daily sweeping. I was proud of my handy work. "Cock a doodle doo! Cock a doodle doo!" I heard Miss Rita's cock cry out. Miss Rita lived on the opposite side to our house about four houses away and as all the cocks in the neighbourhood started to crow in answer to Miss Rita's cock, it was like a musical cock crowing band.

We were on our second to last trip of carrying water when my sister and I started to feel the burn of the sun on our skin. I looked at my big sister with adoration. She was such a beautiful queen everybody loved to look at her and comment about her beauty. She stood five feet tall with a beautiful caramel complexion and long black hair that formed baby-like hair down the sides of her beautiful oval-shaped face. When she smiled her widely spaced teeth added attraction with her striking straight nose that the women in our family liked to boast proudly of, except for me who seemed to have been given only the leftovers.

My hair was mid-length and thick and my complexion dark brown. I had a broad nose that I found fault with and I suffered much ridicule from family and friends who always called me "Broad nose Jackalanton". The only thing that I got complimented for were my beautiful brown eyes. "Jackie hurry up, you are keeping me back."

I tried my best to keep up with the quick strides that Hyacinth made as her body swayed from side to side in the blue loose fitting dress with the torn hemline. Her rubber slippers kicked up dirt at the back of her dress creating a fine film of dust on her calves which appeared as a type of nylon stocking that made her calves shimmer from the different elements of the soil.

"Psst, Psst" She stopped, turned and broke into a small smile. I stumbled a little at her abrupt stop spilling a bit of water on the earth. "Girl, watch where you are going, nah," said Hyacinth, hissing her teeth and rolling her eyes at me as she settled the bucket of water on her head thus calming the slapping sounds the water made as it hit the inside of the bucket from side to side.

I jumped a little when I saw Dalton Edwards appear out of nowhere as a ghost and my big sister started blushing. I was a bit annoyed at this unannounced interruption but it seemed as though it had my sister glowing. Dalton Edwards was our neighbour and Mrs. Elva Edward's grandson who had come from Trinidad to spend a while in Tobago. He was a highly skilled new mechanic so he got work at the bus station.

Mrs. Elva Edwards was very proud of her Trinidadian grandson. All the girls in the village were quite smitten with him and would all seem to swoon when he was around. He was about six feet tall, well-built, light skinned and had soft curly hair, straight nose, thin lips and a gap in the middle of his perfect set of white teeth.

"Wait here!" my sister instructed me as she took the bucket down from her head and made her way to Dalton. This was our morning ritual for the past three months – her spending at least ten minutes in the track leading up the hill to our home talking to Dalton since they had been together at the dance; since Auntie had purchased that beautiful light cream satin cloth and cream lace from the Syrian man that came through our village as a rule every Tuesday. He sold cloth piled high as a mountain on his head.

Auntie who is an excellent seamstress sewed that beautiful Low waist style dress that was in fashion for Hyacinth. She looked beautiful and since then Dalton kept coming around always wanting to make friends. "Morning Jackie," Dalton said to me but I ignored him, steupsed and rolled my eyes at him giving him a view of my back, hands on the bucket, tapping my feet impatiently on the ground. "Girl, cut yuh stupidness out and rest the bucket down and wait," said Hyacinth as she gave me a quick buff.

I felt a quick jab of shame about the way she spoke to me. In my embarrassment I quickly stopped and moved a bit further away. They were both speaking in hushed tones to each other but as boredom started to fill me they did not realize that I had inched closer to hear their conversation. Dalton said, "Tantie come yet?" Hyacinth replied with a soft "no".

"Tantie?" I said to myself, "We ain't have no Tantie coming by us for any visit and besides that the aunts on our father's side, we don't have any relations with them. We just don't speak to them." I spied out of the corner of my eyes as I saw Dalton shoulders droop along with his head as though the world of worries came down on him. I just assumed that he was upset because Tantie didn't come by our house. Stupid Trinidadian, he doesn't even know our family business. None of our 'tanties' will even dare to come by our Auntie Gertie's house anyway.

Hyacinth was in the little outside kitchen making breakfast. The smell of the delicious roast bake and fried jacks opened up my appetite and had my mouth watering along with the grumbling sounds of my stomach. I saw that my aunt was at her sewing machine hustling to finish sew a dress for one of her customers. I approached her still thinking of the conversation which I had overheard earlier between my sister and Dalton about my aunty coming, knowing that my Aunty Gertie didn't like the aunts on my father's side. Oh how I couldn't stand those bacchanalish aunts and I didn't want them to take Hyacinth and me to live with them.

"Aunty, can I ask you something?"

She said, "Jackie, what you want to ask me? Hurry up and ask me. I have to finish up my sewing before this woman come for her dress."

"Aunty, I heard that one of my aunty is coming. Is that true?"

"Jackie, where did you hear that stupidness?"

I was so relieved by her answer knowing that I didn't like my aunties on my father's side. Well, I paused for a while and then told her how I heard Dalton asking Hyacinth if our auntie come as yet. "What you say?" she asked. I told her again.

The look on my auntie's face was enough to fill my heart with fear. It looked as though she was about to collapse and pass out. "Child, run quick and bring me a cup of water." So it was really true then tantie was really coming. Minutes passed as different expressions passed on my auntie's face. "Call your sister for me." I called out to Hyacinth and she came in to the room. It was filled with tension and I was really starting to get frightened. "Jackie, go outside in the

kitchen and wait. I want to speak to your sister alone." Curiosity filled me as I pretended to close the outside kitchen door, then I tiptoed back to eavesdrop on the conversation. "So Madame, when were you going to tell me that you breeding easy so in my house? What shame you putting in my house. When you get pregnant?" Hyacinth? Pregnant? My heart leaped with fright. So that was what was meant by "Tantie coming". Oh it finally dawned on me that Hyacinth didn't see her menses. "Oh God! Oh Lord! Help me! Look at my troubles." I heard my auntie cry and groan as a broken woman. She wept bitterly. "Oh Hyacinth, how could you? I promised your mother I'll take care of you. Why you did that?" I spied through the crease in the board house and saw the tears running down both their faces as Hyacinth stood still weeping not saying anything to our aunt.

As the weeks flew by Hyacinth's stomach grew and she gained a lot of weight and aunty had to purchase more cloth from Mr Aboud. It was so ironic that this cloth-selling man's fabrics played such a huge role in our lives. "Miss Gertie, how are you today? I have some nice new cloth here and buttons to go with it. Come and see what you want."

"Ah coming." Auntie Gertie came off the sewing machine in anticipation of seeing the fabrics that Mr Aboud had brought to sell to her.

Mr Aboud took down his tall mountain of fabrics from his head and untied his bundle and showed her the fabrics. Auntie Gertie said, "Mr Aboud them nice clothes that I does make does get people in real trouble you know. My niece in the house dey ah breed easy on me. So now ah have to buy cloth to sew new clothes for she to look good because niggagram go say she ah big time seamstress and can't sew new clothes for she big belly niece. Ah go well put she out so they go hush up their mouth when they see how good she look. They done crucify me ah ready and done say me ah mine people business and don't know what going on in my house. Well, I go at least show the badmouth bastard them that ah know what coming out ah fuh mi house look darn good. Let them take that and put it in their pipe and smoke it because if me start to talk out people business here many people ah go have to kill people here. And it go have funeral here for weeks to come in this here village and the most cloth you Aboud go sell go be black.

"So let them doh test me patience. Mih niece ah not the only one for breed and she lay with only one body. That good for nothing sly Trini he done gone on back on Tobago SSS, back to Trinidad. Ah hear he get big work down they and ah plan fuh marry another girl after he done teck for me niece virginity and leave she with belly for me to mind."

I could see that Aunty Gertie starting to get angry as the volume of her voice increased with her hand placed on her hips and her large bosom heaving up and down as though she was getting ready to fight. Then she shouted at the top of her voice, looking down at the household she hated the most. "Elvira! Elvira! You wicked old dog. You look at what me have to go through."

She inched closer to the edge of the hill to start to give old Ms Elvira a sound tongue lashing about she no-good family and the worthless grandson that she have who went back to Trini easy easy so. This is to make it look as though he ain't had nothing to do with Hyacinth's belly. "Don't forget to bring the nice lily white diaper cloth and plenty baby pins to go with them for me eh. You hear me – when you come up next week from Trinidad."

Our household turned back to the old calmness with me now having to carry all of the water and sweeping all of the yard. Hyacinth now had the duties of keeping the house clean, cooking, and washing the clothes. I had now grown accustomed to go by myself in the semi-darkness carrying water for the household.

It was a cool Sunday evening when Hyacinth said that she wasn't feeling so well and started vomiting. I alerted Aunty about what was going on as she was in her room resting from being up late into the night sewing by lamp light with her brand new Singer sewing machine. "Jackie, run up the road and call Miss Velma and tell she to come quick. Ah feel the baby coming." Fear and excitement mingled in my heart as I flew down the hill as though I had wings. In no time I was at Miss Velma's house panting and huffing telling her that the baby was coming.

The Christening
(Chrisan Daniel)

Maudica and her husband Joshua were both in their bedroom getting dressed to go to church to stay for their godchild together. It was 7:00 a.m. and the sound of the first church bells started ringing out, signalling to the soon-to-be church goers who attended the Methodist church in the village of Les Coteaux, that church would start in the next hour. "Joshua, how ah look?" Maudica casually asked her husband, as she gave herself a critical look-over in the mirror. She tucked her black bra strap away from sight, turning this way and that in her baby blue, calf length dress with its caped elbow length sleeves. She had finished off the outfit with ash-grey dinner stockings and her sensible black pumps. "Oh shocks, like ah nearly forget meh hat!" she exclaimed, as her husband sat on the bed to tie his shoe laces.

"Girl, you is something else, yes. You know how long I ain't see you so excited," Joshua casually told his wife, as she jauntily placed her white broad-brimmed hat on her head.

Maudica hurriedly told her husband, "Don't forget to walk with enough money to give offering and to contribute to the baby and put on some Ole Spice cologne on your clothes and you ready. And take this." She held out to him a deep blue handkerchief with light brown lines running along the borders.

"Thanks," he said.

Maudica continued, "You know, as godmother, I am the one who have to carry the baby to the church and long face Charmaine vex, because she is the one who get to bring back the baby from the reception for we light lunch. Me ent know why she nuh keep she pauper-self quiet because ah me who buy the baby clothes and the jet beads to put on the baby and you well spend money to buy food and drinks, so them other rest of godparents should know their place because they don't have one cent to give for the christening.

Maudica and her husband pulled up in front of Louisa's house to collect her and baby James who was a happily plumped three-month old baby with soft curly dark brown hair and light brown eyes and skin looking like a white man's. Maudica sat proudly in the front seat of her husband's motor car. There were only two cars in the village and of the two, theirs was the grander. They also had a big house, well-furnished and with electricity. "Blow the horn let she know that we reach." Maudica spoke to her husband in an instructive tone. As he unwillingly obeyed her command, under his breath he spoke the words, "Yes, bossy Miss Maudica."

"What the hell you just say dey under your dam' breath, Joshua? What wrong with you this morning?

"I answer you and say 'Yes darling' and you like yuh ready to fly on me for saying something nice."

It was about four minutes before Louisa came walking out of the track that led to her house holding baby James, all happy and smiling and looking quite cute and smart in his lily white christening outfit. His mother was dressed in a yellow and white polka dot dress. "Louisa she does move so slow. I want to reach early to get a good front seat before the early old church birds take up the best seat! Shims!" Maudica hissed under her breath.

Maudica proudly walked into the church that was half filled, carefully holding the baby that lay in her arms, half asleep.

The service passed beautifully with the minister blessing the infant and godparents charging them before God and man to be good godparents to help raise baby James the right way, always willing to be on the lookout for negativity that may come his way. All over the congregation were heard responses of "Amen!" "Hallelujah!" "Glory!" "Yes, Reverend!" The service came to an end after collection was taken up and the recessional song, "Greet Somebody in Jesus Name", was sung.

Charmaine, the other godmother, had taken up her responsibility to carry the baby back to the reception for the light lunch. Maudica and her husband had just come out of the church together, when she caught a glimpse of her old school rival Gwendolyn and her face changed. Oh how she couldn't stand that labe-lip woman. "Aye, Joshua, come out of the crowd," Maudica called out to Joshua, signalling him to come over.

Gwendolyn silently waltzed over to where Maudica stood waiting for her husband. "Well yuh finally prove today you is a real mamapool to come and feel that you is the best macome for meh family picknee and you know you like fuh act as though you more quemse than everybody round here," she greeted Maudica nastily.

"Why don't you move yuh mingpiling, sucker guts self from in front of me," Maudica hissed out at Gwendolyn.

Gwendolyn's face changed through the pure insult that was hurled at her. Her face took on a distracted look as she moved closer to Maudica.

"Me ain't have no cause to go an' susu-susu behind your back and what me have to tell you in front of this church is bible 'tory. You have to be the most dotish woman in the whole ah

Tobago fuh come and stay for your husband picknee and acting frontish in front of everybody. Ah laugh you behind your back. It seem like you is the last one to know that your husband does be creeping out of Louisa house on mornings on Mondays and Fridays, every week for the past year and a half."

Maudica's face changed and she felt as though her world was closing in on her. Her chest held her heart in a tight grip and her stomach felt as though a knife was slicing away inside her. How could her husband do this to her? She was a good wife and mother to their two children and for this to happen to her it was considered to be an unpardonable sin.

"Joshua Theophilus Jack, can you excuse yourself from those gentlemen and come here for a few seconds?" Hmmmm, she grumbled to herself. Maudica was fuming. All of her emotions were cooking at an extremely high temperature and she was almost ready to blow out all that high pressure steam of emotions.

"What happen to you, woman? Meh just left you good good and talking to them men and now in less than three minutes, your whole temperament change? Meh find you does overdo it with them hoggish behaviour that you like fuh show off."

Suddenly Joshua stopped talking. He looked at his wife, Maudica. She had fixed him with a stony stare. A cold wave washed over him. The hurt of his betrayal was in her eyes. He understood the look. She knew.

'labe-lip' – long bottom lip   'susu-susu' – gossip quietly
'mamapool' – stupid person   'bible story' – the truth
'quemse' – highfaluting; pompous   'dotish' – foolish
'mingpiling' – miserly   'frontish' – showy
'sucker guts' – poor and hungry

Maria Bristol

Maria Bristol-Darlington was born in Trinidad but made her home in Tobago sometime later, having moved there with her parents. She started writing at the tender age of eight. She credits her love for writing to her love for reading.

Some of her early works included poems, jingles, essays and short stories. She has been a primary school teacher for over thirty-three years. She has one sister and two brothers and is the 'baby' of the family. She is the proud mother of three children: two sons and a daughter and a grandmother of three.

She writes on a variety of themes, but religious ones are her specialty. She has composed several pieces for church functions that cater for children. She now writes speeches, poems and short stories. She holds a Bachelor of Education in Language Arts and is currently pursuing her Masters in Health Promotion at the University of the West Indies.

AGING WITH DIGNITY
(MARIA BRISTOL)

So yuh tink yuh cud treat me any ole way?
Ah hope yuh realize yuh go reach here one day!
Ah old now so yuh tink ah so derelict and useless,
And yuh at yuh peak so yuh deserve only de best!
Who tell yuh ah want to live in home for de age?
After ah wuk hard, build me home and always manage!
So yuh put me here well outta yuh sight,
And do yuh duty by visiting once every fortnight!
Then all yuh collecting me hard earn pension,
Force me to sign it and not a red cent pass me vision!
Yuh love to talk down to me as if ah is ah little child,
Shouting as if ah deaf and cussing me all de while!
Yet when yuh bring yuh big time friends and we family to visit
Yuh hugging and kissing me and in de seat of honour ah sit!
Why yuh tink yuh have to treat me as a nuisance?
And to yuh tune yuh always expect me to dance?
Long ago de elderly was treated with respect and dignity,
But nowadays we treated with only contempt and pity!
In de past if yuh go to a function or ride in a bus,
Ah youth wud give de elderly dey seat without ah fuss!
But dat ent happening now at all, at all, at all.

Dey ent even care if de older person stand til dey fall!
Back to yuh: Fuh birthdays and mothers' day ah get treated like ah queen,
But fuh all the 363 other days, ah is treated as ah ole "has-been!"
Ah sure when ah dead, yuh go play dat yuh bawling,
All dem church people yuh go be wuking on impressing!
Big wake, repast, casket, wreaths galore and glowing tributes,
As if de dead cud appreciate yuh "bigging-up" dey attributes!
When ah alive yuh treating me like dirt,
By subjecting me to all kinda abuse, pain and hurt!
Beware yuh ent end up like me – forgotten, forsaken and neglected,
If yuh ent change yuh attitude, yuh own bad treatment will be expected.
Unless yuh expect to die young; ole age will be yuh lot too,
Someone guh rob yuh of yuh dignity like yuh now do!
So my dear young people, take some time out to reflect,
And remember growing ole guh also be yuh prospect!
So yuh better practise de ole saying dat's tried and true:
"Always do unto others as yuh'll have dem do unto yuh!"

Composed on 24 September, 2014

DEDICATED TO ALL WORKAHOLICS
(MARIA BRISTOL)

I thought of having a day off to rest
But it wasn't my birthday
So I thought I'd let it wait,
Because there was so much still to be done.

I thought of having a day off to rest,
But it wasn't Father's or Mother's Day,
So I thought I'd let it wait
Because there was work that had to be done.

I thought of having a day off to rest,
But it wasn't my Anniversary,
So I thought I'd let it wait
Because my schedule was still too tight.

I thought of having a day off to rest
But it wasn't a public holiday,
So I thought I'd let it wait
Because the time just was not right.

Well you finally got the time off to rest,
It was a very special day!
It was your funeral!
You had finally burnt yourself out!
So now you rest for eternity.

MISUNDERSTOOD
(Maria Bristol)

Wait! I can't believe what I see.
You really shunning and
scorning me?
I didn't always have this
disease, you know!
I didn't go out and get it just
so!
I was a happily married wife,
I thought I had the perfect
life!
Until my husband started to
stray,
And now he has come to rue
that day!
He knock around from pillar
to post.
A lifestyle that made him
give up the ghost!
He gone and leave me now
to suffer,
Branded with this dreadful
HIV/AIDS stigma.
People shunning me and my
children,
Leaving us without one
single friend.

I lose my job, no-one want
me around,
That's why I begging all
round town!
I don't have money for food
or treatment,
My problems have robbed
me of every cent.
What will become of my
children when I'm dead?
Lord, how that thought
hurting my head!
I always tried to be a good
person,
But my spouse liked having
outside fun!
So he end up tainting my
whole life,
Into my heart he thrust a
fatal knife!
So who are you to stand in
judgment?
You better ask the Lord to
help you repent!
Remember what you do to
one, the least like me,

Don't you know you do unto
Thee!
So search deep within your
uncaring heart,
And from your
discrimination depart.
Say but for the grace of God,
there go I!
Thank God for His mercies
by and by.
Remember God came to
heal and save,
His only Son He so freely gave.
Keep a Christian thought
within your head
Show brotherly and sisterly
love instead.
You don't know one thing
about my past,
So don't turn up your nose
and run by fast!
Remember I am a human
being too,
One who can be hurt by
what you say and do!
So stop the stigma of HIV/
AIDS discrimination
That is slowly destroying our
beautiful nation.

THE SEA AT NIGHT
(Maria Bristol)

I don't hear you from a distance,
But as I draw close you acknowledge my presence,
With a thud and a deafening roar
Your waves crashing onto the shore.

Always in motion, never constant
Thundering! Then calm in an instant!
Salty spray filling the night's air
From your waters that are crystal clear.

When I visit you at night,
Stars and moon shed their light
Causing my shadow to be cast
Oh! How I wish it would all last!

I try to look beyond your horizon,
But after all has been said and done,
Your vastness is so very awesome,
To swim in your waters, I feel welcome!

But you may dash me against some stones,
And break my already fragile bones!
So, I'm comfortable with the distance we keep
And I'll dream of your warmness when I'm asleep.

$\mathcal{H}$elen Louise Nathan

HELEN NATHAN explains that, "coming from a small family unit of father, mother and two girls, I grew up as an only child, as my older sister was married and out of the home by the time I was six years old. I grew up with a very protective mother and in her tendency to want to shield me from danger and harm, it meant a lot of restrictions on the amount of interaction I had with other children. School, of course, curtailed some of that.

Within my school years, I participated in the Arts Festivals, in verse and choral speaking, poetry reading and public speaking competitions. There was also a radio station set up at school in which I was asked to be an announcer. But still there was that imbedded personality that saw me in my early years remaining on the outside, and looking in or observing others, their mannerisms, their reactions, hearing what people said, but also hearing what they did not say, or moreso, seeing the contradiction between what is said with the month and what was said with the eyes.

I am quiet but not an introvert. I have looked at the close knit family of days gone by and the equally close knit neighbourhoods. I have seen the changes in family life and the disintegration of both the home and community and its impact on the society as a whole. I am very often led to put pen to paper, therefore, to comment andor to give what I hope is the remedy to our plight."

AN OPEN HEART
(Helen Nathan)

You have erected barriers against the darts and arrows
life throws at you.
You have dug your trenches and built your forts
And that might seem rightly so, for so often you have
found yourself between a rock and a hard place,
afraid to let your defences down.
Sure that it would only bring you pain, and there is nought
but that to gain--if you offer your heart to - LOVE - that
insane game.

But tell me is there not more to it than just a game?
With winners and losers, and points scored, for and against
—
the hurt and the hurting?
What about openness and trust – the giving and sharing,
which is the essence of love.
What about honesty and purity of heart and soul?
What about loyalty and faithfulness?

My friend why so easily we believe and accept the baser
qualities--
Court and pamper the darker side of our nature?
How quickly we lean to the selfish.
We move backward instead of forward ---
Will tear down instead of uplift
Will see the worst not the best, will criticize instead of praise
Will close the door of our heart instead of open it.

BREAKDOWN THOSE WALLS AROUND YOUR HEART!

Lift the gates and let someone share your dreams and hopes.
Open your arms and say welcome to life!
Open your heart and give love the chance it deserves!
With an open heart you risk the pains to find the joys.
For if you never dare, you never gain,
If you never give, you cannot hope to receive.

BUILDING BRIDGES
(*Helen Nathan*)

A helping hand, a pleasant
word or two,
A smile, a few minutes of
your time.
A calm reply, a blessing instead
of indifference or a curse.
Seeking the ways of
bonding. Resisting those
that would create disunity.
Saying "Thank you". Letting
someone know you
appreciate him or her.

It takes so little an effort to
build the bridge of
human kindness,
And extend it to a weary fellow
traveller along this rocky
road of life.

A touch of your hand, a
listening ear to show that
you care
Helps lift a little of the load
carried by someone;
Fills its place with hope; stops
someone's headlong rush

down the pathway of
despair;
With your support dispel the
dark cloud of loneliness
in a person's life.
Build the bridge of human
compassion
Build it over the crossroads
of confusion and hurt,
Where so many of us now
exist.
Send a letter make that call,
Never doubt – that old
forgotten friendship,
you may just be able to
mend it.
Extinguish that flame of anger,
Spray it with words of peace.

Build that bridge of
harmony; put it across
the intersection of
discouragement and pain.
It takes no engineering
qualification, no physical
exertion, no schematic plans.

It does not diminish you, is
not harmful to you.
All it takes is the warmth of
a giving heart to
Build bridges of kindness
and support; bridges of peace
and harmony, bridges of
communication and
co-operation.
And ultimately,
understanding hope and love.

Hovis Trim

HOVIS TRIM is Patience Hill born and bred. He has worked at several jobs but his first love is business. He operates a well-stocked grocery at Patience Hill Junction. In between attending to his customers and stocking his shelves, Hovis engages in his second love – that of writing tons and tons of short stories. Hovis can truly write his own book.

A TOBAGO LOVE STORY
by Hovis Trim

This is a story about a young man by the name of Kyle. At the beginning of the story Kyle was about twenty one (21) years old. He was known to the entire village and the police as a common thief, breaking and entering people's property and stealing from them. He was always in and out of prison and sometimes, he got a 'cut tail' from his neighbours.

In the village where Kyle lived, there was one family who treated him well and gave him odd jobs. This family consisted of five people – Josh and Pat, husband and wife, and the children, Ren who was eleven years old, Dwight, five and Trudy, seven. They lived in a three bedroom house and owned a car. Both Josh and Pat worked and the children went to school. Every morning before leaving, Pat would take out all the ingredients to cook dinner when she returned from work in the evening. She would season the meat, cut up the vegetables and do any other preparations so that it would be easier for her later.

One day, a Valentine's Day, Kyle remembered a dream he had had the night before, that Pat had given him a beautiful Valentine's Day gift on behalf of her family. So he wondered, what if the family really has a Valentine's Day gift for me, what do I give them in return? What am I going to give these people who are the only ones that are good to me? Then a thought came to his mind that if he could get into the house, he could clean the bedrooms, wash the dishes, vacuum the floor and do the laundry. Then he said to himself, "Yes I would do it."

So he went to the house and he made sure that he was not being seen. He then proceeded to remove a few louvres from the window at the back of the house and he went inside. While inside the house, Kyle washed the dishes, vacuumed the floor, scrubbed the bathroom, made up the beds in all the rooms and did the laundry.

Finally Kyle was hungry. He opened the fridge but there was nothing to eat right away. He looked around and saw the prepared ingredients Pat had put aside to cook dinner, when she returned from work. Kyle said to himself, "I am going to cook this food for Pat." After he was finished cooking, Kyle went to the living room and using a piece of cardboard and colouring pencils from the children's room, he created a sign that read "Happy Valentine's Day to you all, from Kyle!" And then he left the house through the front door, forgetting to replace the louvre panes that he had removed at the back of the house to get inside.

Later in the evening, the family returned home and upon entering the house, Pat immediately realized something was not right. As she checked the back door, she noticed the missing louvres and right away called out to her husband Josh and went rushing back outside. "Josh someone has broken into our house."

Josh immediately called the police on his mobile phone and Pat went across by her closest neighbour, Miss Jack, and asked her if she had seen anyone by her house during the day. Miss Jack told her that she had seen Kyle at the back door but she did not suspect anything because she thought that Pat was at home and that she had given Kyle an odd job to do around the house. Pat thanked Miss Jack and returned to her house where she informed Josh that it was Kyle who had broken into their home.

After a few minutes the police arrived and were told by Pat that Kyle had been seen by the neighbour at the back door of the house and the police were shown the space where the louvres were missing. The police asked if anything was missing from the house, but Pat told them she had not checked as yet. The police told her to check and see if anything was missing and in the meantime they would go and look for Kyle, who was not too far away. He was at his home sleeping when the police arrived. He was arrested and told what he had been arrested for and he was taken away.

Meanwhile back at the family house they were stunned to see what Kyle had done. The bathroom was scrubbed, the floor was vacuumed, the laundry washed, the dishes also washed and the beds made up and the family dinner cooked. Pat was so impressed with Kyle's cooking that she whispered, "Where did Kyle learn to cook like this?"

The family got another shock of their lives when Trudy called out, "Mom, Dad, come see this." It was the sign that Kyle had written "Happy Valentine's Day to you all, from Kyle!" Pat immediately broke down in tears and while she was being comforted by Josh, she said to him, "How could we do this to Kyle? He meant well. He did all of this for us and now he is in jail."

Josh said, "Let's see if we can get him out."

The family came up with a plan that would certainly help Kyle. They told the police that it was not Kyle who had broken into their home; it was instead a very close family member who wanted to give them a surprise Valentine's Day gift by doing all the chores, but had to remove the louvres in order to get inside the house. The police believed their story and Kyle was set free.

The next day, Kyle was in for the shock of his life after he related to the family what caused him to do what he did. He was hugged by the family, kissed by the kids, most of all. He nearly passed away with shock when Josh said to him, "Kyle, since you did all that for us as a Valentine's Day gift, we are going to give you your Valentine's Day gift. Would you come and live with us?"

"What, are you serious?" asked Kyle.

"Please say yes," teased Dwight.

A stunned Kyle just stood there in awe. "I need to think about this!" he said.

"No problem," replied Josh, "but we need your answer in two days."

"Okay!" said Kyle, as he left for his home.

Two days later, Kyle appeared at the door of the family's house and rang the bell, which was answered by Dwight. "Please say yes!" said Dwight. Kyle smiled and said "Yes, little brother. It is yes".

Dwight hugged Kyle and quickly called out to his mom and dad. "It's Kyle and he said yes!" screamed Dwight. There was a great joy in the house at the time as Kyle was warmly accepted by the family.

Kyle was quickly enrolled in an institution by Josh to do joinery. A few years passed and Kyle had changed his ways and he was now admired and loved by the community, including the police who visited him regularly to see how he was doing.

He eventually graduated from the institution with a certificate thus becoming a certified joiner.

After five years, Kyle found the right girl and was encouraged by Pat and Josh to marry her. A few months afterwards another addition was made to the family. Kyle's wife gave birth to a son. This brought great joy to the family, especially to Pat and Josh who said that this child was their first grandchild.

Kyle eventually turned out to be the best joiner in the community and everyone loved him. He was loved so much in the community that the residents named the street where he lived "KYLE STREET."

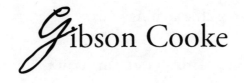

BITTER SWEET…18
By Gibson Cooke

ACT 1

(Jean is in a jubilant mood. She is singing and dancing to the popular tune, "Brok, brok, brok it up." Unnoticed, her friend Ann enters the room with an envelope, takes a seat and looks on curiously.)

Ann: Like you practising for Carnival! You know how long ah watching you?

Jean: Nah! Girl, ah just can't wait till tomorrow.

Ann: What happening tomorrow?

Jean: You forget? Tomorrow is meh birthday!!

Ann: Oh yes is true. So you keeping a party?

Jean: Nah, ah go be 18 years old tomorrow. I will be my own woman. Free to do what I want and go and come as I please.

Ann: Is so?

Jean: Yes, when you 18, you is an adult. Free to do anything you want.

Ann: Next year I go be 18 too. But I don't think you does be free as they say.

Jean: How you mean?

Ann: Well some parents does want to put you out.

Jean: That only apply to boys, not to girls.

Ann: You think so?

Jean: I know what ah saying. Parents can't put out girl children just so. Remember the law is for woman and not for man!

Ann: If I was you I wouldn't think so!

Jean: Anyhow, the first thing ah doing tomorrow is go and put a stud on meh tongue and put on a tattoo.

Ann: Where you getting the money to do that?

Jean: You know how long ah saving up for that!!

Ann: Girl I can't do them things in my father house. I will have to find some where to go.

Jean: Your father is ah old timer.

Ann: Well he done tell me he don't mind the ear ring, chain and ras but not the nails, tattoo and studs.

Jean: So you go let your father tell you what to do with your body?

Ann: Not really but he say when ah woman do them things, they cursing God.

Jean: Well let me see if anybody could stop me.

Jean's mom emerges from the bedroom.

Mother: I in there listening to everything you saying.

Jean: So what of that?

Mother: That is all the ambition you have?

Jean: So what so wrong in putting on a tattoo or piercing your tongue?

Mother: Is true nobody could stop you because is your body and you free to do what you want, but you wouldn't be staying here.

Jean: We go see.

Mother; I thought you woulda go and look for something to do or take some lessons. You waste five years in school.

Jean: I waste my time in school?

Mother:	What papers you bring home? Eh? Alyuh have things so easy. These days dey paying alyuh to learn.
Jean:	Is everybody head could take book?
Mother:	Is better to try and fail than fail to try!
Jean:	Mammy, me eh taking you on at all!!
Mother:	You know everything you could do when you 18 but ain't know that the minding stop!
Jean:	Ok. Ah go look for something to do.
Mother:	Where you go find work without papers? CEPEP?
Jean:	CEPEP? Me aint working by no roadside in no hot sun for no little bit ah money. Ah bound to find something better.
Ann:	Anyhow ah bring two set of forms for you. *(She takes out some forms and hands them to Jean).*
Jean:	Forms for what?
Ann:	These are for courses at the Hotel School and these to apply for nursing.
Jean:	Me! I aint workng in nobody kitchen neither I aint dressing nobody sore foot!
Ann:	Well they picking for police next week. We could try dat.
Jean:	If you want you could try them but not me!
Ann:	Girl, the salary good and is ah Government work!
Jean:	Well I ain't going and lock up nobody. Police work is dog work!!!

Ann:	Girl, leh we give them a try and forget about the tattoo and studs and them things. All that could come after.
Jean:	All you and Mammy trying to do is hot up meh head!
Mother:	From what I see, all you intend to do is go in town and hustle.
Jean:	Hah! I know how you thinking.
Mother:	Anyhow, ah warning you in front yuh friend when you catch belly or sickness, don't bring them here.
Jean:	Belly or sickness! Where ah getting them from? Is ring on meh finger before anything else. What you take me for?
Mother:	Ah hope yuh mean what you say.
Ann:	*(Getting up)* Ah sorry I go out of my way to help you because ah thought you was meh friend!
Jean:	Help me!! I could handle meh own stories.
Ann:	Ok. Well I gone.

ACT II

(Newton and his friend enter the Port View Bar to take a drink and Newton is shocked to see his sister Jean behind the bar.)

Jean:	Good evening, Sir.
Newton:	Don't 'sir' me at all!
Jean:	Well you is meh big brother so ah have to show you respect.
Newton:	Respect in a bar! Look, give me two beers.

(They collect their beers and retreat to a corner).

Friend:	Dat is not your sister Jean?

Newton: She self!

Friend: She really change up, ah nearly didn't make she out.

Newton: Well she is a big woman now and on she own.

Friend: Of all the places, is here she end up?

Newton: Well if is that she choose, what you want me to do?

Friend: Ah really surprise at she!

Newton: Last week ah went to see Mammy and she tell me Jean pack she bags and ride out. But ah didn't know is here she end up!

Friend: So you couldn't help she get something better?

Newton: Yes ah talk to the boss and he promise to pull she in because the cleaner woman going home next month.

Friend: That go be good.

(While conversing, Newton is fascinated at the way Jean is fraternizing with the patrons especially a group of girls in a corner. Newton goes to the bar again).

Jean: What can I do for you?

Newton: Give me another round of beers. So you working here now?

Jean: Yes!

Newton What time you finish working?

Jean: *(Looking at the clock on the wall)* Next fifteen minutes.

Newton: Well ah want to have a talk with you.

Jean: No problem.

(Jean has finished her shift and goes to her brother and friend with two beers in hand. Newton attempts to pay for them).

Jean: Is all right, I paid for them already.

(Jean takes a seat with them).

Newton: How long you working here now?

Jean: About a month now.

Newton: Mammy know this?

Jean: Well ah tell she ah get a work and a place to stay!

Newton: She know is in a bar you working?

Jean: I didn't tell she where ah working. The important thing is that ah working!

Newton: You shame to tell she you working in a bar?

Jean: Shame! So what wrong with working in a bar?

Newton: Ok, ok. Well, the cleaner woman in the Department going home next month so ah talk to the boss about you.

Jean: And what he say?

Newton: He say let you come and check him.

Jean: Well, tell him ah not interested. Them bossman does want you to work for your money twice!

Friend: Girl, the work easy; is only two hours ah day you have to work. They making you permanent one time. The pay good and you getting holidays, sick leave, casual leave and they even have a health plan.

Jean: I good where ah is right here! The pay good and ah does get ah day off every week. Don't talk about the tips. Sometimes they does be more than meh pay!

Newton:	So you not interested then?

Jean:	No!

Friend:	Newton, if is so I will talk to my sister.

Newton:	Another thing; Ah notice you mixing up with them girls over there.

Jean:	So what! Dem is meh good friends.

Newton:	You know what is their reputation?

Jean:	What reputation? Is dem that get this work for me and all ah we shack up!

Newton:	Girl, you really gone to the cleaners.

Jean:	*(Getting vex, jumps up).* So you and all telling me how to live my life? To hell with you!

(Jean grabs her bag and goes across and joins her girlfriends).

Act lll

(Newton enters the house with a package. He hugs his mother and kisses her.)

Newton:	Happy birthday, Mammy.

Mother:	Well boy, I say alyuh throw me away!

Newton:	Oh gosh Mammy, how ah go do you dat?

Mother:	Since morning ah looking out for you.

Newton:	Ah couldn't come before, ah had to finish some work in the office first.

(He hands his mother the package)

Mother: Is what?

Newton: Open and you will see!

(She opens it and takes out a dress. She hugs him.)

Mother: Thanks! Thanks!

Newton: You don't have to thank me. Is my duty.

(Newton takes out his wallet and gives his mother money.)

Newton: If you don't like it or it don't fit, you could carry it back and change it. Anything extra I will pay.

Mother: So how is Susan and them children?

Newton: Them better than me. You will see them this evening they planning to give you a surprise.

(They both sit down)

Newton: Mammy, how you and Jean getting along.

Mother: Boy she suddenly pick up a speed liming every night and sleeping whole day. When I talk to she about it she pack she bag and ride out. I don't know which part of the world she is.

Newton: She right here in Tobago!

Mother: Eh heh?

Newton: Yes, ah went in a bar in town and bounce she up.

Mother: So is in a bar she end up?

Newton: She not only working in a bar but she link up with some lesbian girls.

Mother: Oh my gosh. Well she gone to the cleaners.

Newton: And you know ah get a work for she and she bluntly refuse it!

Mother: Well she really did tell me she is a big woman now and she could handle she own stories.

Newton: So if you want to see she when you go in town, check out the Port View bar.

Mother: Well I ain't go see she because I don't go in bars.

(*Ann enters*)

Ann: Morning Miss Mabel, morning Newton.

(*They both answer*)

Ann: Miss Mabel, where Jean?

Mabel: Girl since she leave here, I aint see she again. Is she brother who just tell me that she working in a bar in town.

Ann: Ah just come to tell she that ah get through with police and I have to start training next week.

Mabel: Girl I over glad to hear that!

Ann: Thanks Miss Mabel, but I have a problem.

Mabel: What is that?

Ann: They also call me to start training as a nurse.

Mabel: Well, girl, like you go have to split up yourself.

Newton: Ah glad to hear that too but you is the one to choose for yourself.

Ann: Ah think I will do the nursing. That will keep me out of the eyes of the public.

Mabel: Is a pity Jean didn't take you advice.

Newton: Well she prefer the bright lights. I don't know what benefit she will get from that.

Mabel: That child really let me down.

(*At this point, the front door is pushed open to show Jean slumped in a wheel chair. Two girls are pushing the chair.*

Both girls: Miss Mabel, we bring your daughter for you!

They both leave hurriedly. Miss Mabel, Newton and Ann surround the wheelchair and look at Jean with shock. Mabel rushes to the door shouting after the girls who do not answer.

Mabel: Hello! Hello! (She turns to Jean) What the hell I seeing here!! Girl you very sick!

Newton: Sick! You aint see is a corpse they bring for you. What a birthday present!

(They *keep shaking and calling Jean but there is no response. Mabel empt*ies the black plastic bag which was on Jean's lap and two pieces of clothing fall out.)

Mabel: Look alyuh try and call the ambulance.

Newton: I don't think the hospital does take in them kinds ah people.

Mabel: We have to try and find somewhere to put she.

Newton: And who go pay the bill? I already have wife and children to see about.

Mabel: Well she can't stay here because I can't see about she in that condition.

Ann: Well if that is what a nurse have to put up with, ah change mih mind, ah go be ah police woman instead.

Mabel: Boy, what we go do?

Newton: Try and pray and let God take she life soon. I will spend the money to bury she!

Mabel: And if she don't dead now?

Ann: Miss Mabel, Miss Mabel go to the Welfare people, they will send somebody to see bout she.

Mabel: How long dat does take?

Ann: Ah don't know but they will send somebody.

(*Mabel looks at Jean*)

Mabel: Girl you didn't last as long as a snow cone. You talk about live fast, die young and make a beautiful corpse. Well you go be the ugliest copse I ever will see.

(The three *lift Jean from the wheelchair and take her to the bedroom.*)

$\mathcal{J}$ana Moses

Jana is highly regarded for her realistic depictions of life daily struggle occasionally using humorous colloquial speech.

Growing up in the small village of Argyle, Tobago in a single parent household has helped to shape her views and philosophy on life that she portrays in her lyrical pieces. Her work mostly comprises of themes surrounding motherhood, love, sexuality, peace and humanity. A mother of one and a single parent herself, Jana knows how to "keep it real" and truly connect with her audience.

A former student of Author Lok Jack School of Continuing Studies, her passion for writing started eight years ago when her father, a Trinidadian writer and calypsonian, passed away. She believes her father's gift was passed on to her so she could understand what had engulfed his world. Now she has blossomed into nothing less than a tasteful talent. Her collection consists of several poems and she is now exploring the field of song writing.

In 2009, she founded *Mood Writers*, an online forum for poets and writers to share their work with like-minded people. She has organised and performed at several shows in Tobago and Trinidad under the stage-name *Modern Day Hippie*.

Why Do I Love You?

(Jana Moses)

Some questions should have an answer,
Like –
What's your favourite colour?
Where do you see yourself in five years?
Do you like broccoli?

Some questions lead to personal opinion,
Like –
Was Michael Jackson murdered?
How do you feel about our Government?
Do you think I'm cute?

But there're some questions one would see no reason to answer
Like –
What colour is wind?
What really causes you to dance?
Why do I love you?

Why, do I love you?
Frankly, it's rhetorical!

At the seriousness of it, behind all reason of it, it's not at all comedic
Yet I laugh
For I know why I like you, but I am dumbfounded by LOVE, and the fact that you asked.
It is a question modelled not to elicit a specific answer, unlike the famous "Do I love you?"
To which my answer would be, "Yes!" and my actions would determine this is true.

But "Why" dictates to my aura, infects my sanity, messes with my health
The guilty pleasure questioning the inevitable, I smile at the confusion trying to understand too, myself.
Yet, without motive, allows me to show the ultimate point of view
This, my most powerful reflex emotion towards you
Recognize I love you… just because …. I do

It somehow has wings, for I feel I could fly
It has a voice as powerful as a lion's roar, filled with pride
So it is beyond my human nature
My human nature
Mine… Not yours
I can't say why I love you, but loving you brings me joy

"Why" equals reasons
Which I'd let go
To let it dance with the universe, and let destiny flow.
When it comes back I embrace it with faith,
And hope that the same love is reciprocated and not hate

Be blessed by the cosmic essence of my soul as well simultaneously see
I LOVE YOU, so don't question it.
With regards,
Me.

We are the Wrongs

By Jana Moses

Too much crying
Too much dying
Too much lying
Pretending we don't see
Too much twisting the truth for murders to go free
More deaths in the streets
Gangs making a mock
Places where I learn to creep
I'm now afraid to walk
Yet we pass the blame, amidst ole talk.

The more things change, the more they stay the same
Households and parliament re-arrange
Segregation remains
No one for all
Another day by the gun a young man fall
Mother holds her head and bawl, Johnny was a good boy
But when Johnny was one year old he had a plastic gun for a toy
Tell me, where Johnny get that gun from?

Time for we to take responsibility for the circumstances we breed
It takes a village to raise a child
What happen to that creed?
Now it's all about the race
No equality in finding one's place
But with fake smiles on our face
We act like we don't see
That we are the wrongs in our country.

Kleon Mcpherson

KLEON McPHERSON who hails from the beautiful island of Tobago, brings a refreshing and innovative style to spoken word with his intellectual poetic humor and remarkable lyrical speed and word play. His distinctive intonations and delivery makes him one of Trinidad and Tobago's premiere Spoken Word artists. He is well known for participating in the widely successful Spoken Word programme, the Free Speech Project, which airs on TTRN- Trinidad and Tobago Radio Network Limited (96.1fm, 94.7fm and 107.7fm).

The originality and creativity of his pieces, which can be heard on the You Tube website, makes him stand out from his counterparts. He continues to captivate audiences across the country and has been featured at Machel Monday 2014. One of his pieces entitled 'A Hot Shh' was actually listed as number one on the indigenous song charts.

McPherson is not only an astounding poet, but has also extensively contributed to the sphere of culture, being a stilt walker, virtuoso pan player, carnival band leader, cultural researcher and international presenter. He has never lost sight of his educational pursuits possessing a Bachelor of

Arts Degree in History and also a Master of Arts in Cultural Studies with distinction. He hopes that his work not only provides a form of entertainment but also enables audiences to be enlightened, inspired and to receive some sort of a message.

Mr. Steel Pan
(Kleon McPherson)

Oh, Mr Steel Pan, your evolution could not have been stranger, than your initial manifestation as an empty biscuit container. You were crafted and moulded by African hands, observed pre-maturely accompanying tam-boo bamboo bands. I knew some of your founding fathers, like Ellie Mannette and Winston Spree, and at the spectacle known as carnival you are displayed in all your glee. No one can ever attest that your transition was not profound, from a simply percussion instrument to a stylistic concave oil drum. Several of your octaves emulate the acclaimed piano and your harmonious sounds can be heard emanating from your birth place of Trinidad and Tobago. Your extensive tonal range creates a distinctive aura, which can only be experienced through a steel orchestra. At your event identified as Panorama, an epic Spartan battle can be revealed, where your warriors are uniformly attired, with mallets in hand, behind chromed shields. Globally, your existence can be noted as legendary, for being the greatest acoustic instrument invented in the 20th century.

$\mathcal{T}$risha Leander

"What comes out of a man defiles him". With great abilities and a spirit of success, I, Trisha Camia Leander, was born in Tobago on 31st July 1978. I grew up and was educated in Trinidad. I presently reside in Tobago with my dear husband and my four amazing children.

By profession I am a Business/Spanish teacher. I have earned my BSc. in Management Studies and a Post Graduate Diploma in Education.

By purpose my endowments are in the Arts. I am passionate about words expressed through poetry, quotes, songs, monologues, stories. I am also skilled with my hands indulging in fashion, art, crafts, cuisine. Dancing is also on my agenda. Sounds like a lot.

When one does what comes naturally, one is kept alive as if with oxygen; one is unaware of time passing, and one experiences a sense of completion: satisfying.

Deep in thought, mostly strategizing and allowing my creative juices to flow is like heaven. If I am to sum up myself in one word it would have to be "creative" – simply said.

TOBAGO VILLAGE HUMOUR
(Trisha Leander)

I meet this guy in **Parlatuvier**
At Ms. Louis birthnight
Telling me he is ah **Englishman B** aaaay
Bout he want to take me to some **Bloody Bay**
Well I never
No music ain't playing, but hear he
Buh he want to **L'Anse Fourmi**
He tell me lewwe spend ah weekend at **Charlotte**'s **Vill**a
It would be an experience outta **Speys - side** say

Yuh know I find out he broken to thief
Not even the hotel he could **Del aford**
So ah kick him out de party
An slam Ms. **Louis D'Or**
Ah wanted to pelt him with some **Rox**s **bo rough**
Meh good friend Romain
A rgyle-less friend
Taught me how to **Kendall** the peace
He say think of a **Belle Garden**
A **Rich mond**, playing on a **Glam organ**

All of a sudden Mr. **Pembroke**
Dis time with all he **Goldsborough** ed
Telling me he doh have no money
But he have **Goodwood**
And he will make me feel like I on **Mt. St. George**
And he **Hope**
That I, Ms **John, Dial** he cell number
To make some time for he
So he could get ah **Scarborough**
From he neigh**Bacolet**
Well I never meet ah man so low
Lower than **Lowlands**

He going on and on
How Colette driving ah Honda **BonAccord**
An I **Carnbee** eating and drinking in he friend car
I **Bethel** could fall from his Sup **Plymouth**
Like ah **Canaan** ball
Ah say Mister, what is your **Point**
Pigeon or **Crown**

WHY ABORTION?
(Trisha Leander)

I wonder what mummy's thinking
From inside here
I can hear her heart beating
She seems excited
Excited to see me in another trimester or so
I hear a voice
That must be daddy
He's getting louder
And mummy too
As long as they are together
That don't really bother me
Look, my mummy and daddy going out
No more shouts
I feel a peace
I feel a calm
Now I'm cold
Ooh a massage
I better smile
Get my best side
They are taking my picture
Again
Wow I'm already a movie star
I've got hopes and dreams
And purpose
Endless possibilities
Another room, another bed
This must be a hotel

I hear snickers
Mummy is crying
She must be vex
Of my sex
I couldn't help that
Better luck next… time

I hear an orchestra
Instruments
Or cutlery

What was that
I swear something just touched me
Get a grip of yourself child

What, what was that
I know I felt it for real this time
And it hurts
Mummy, can you hear me
Daddy can you help me
I can't understand
Help me

Well I must be dead and gone to heaven
St. Peter meet me by the gate
Lead me to a place for children like me
Unwanted, unborn, un-whatever
I see them looking at me
Looking like me and not looking like me
I see them in singles, twins, triplets

And 'ets' that I've never heard of before
All of us have the same question
The same look on our face

We want to know Why
Why you never asked us what we wanted
Why you believe we must be aborted
Without thought
Another life unplugged
Like euthanasia
Murdered like many Youths in Asia
To be haunted and taunted
Disappointed
By the memories of the memories
You will never have
Wondering what would have been
My eye colour
My hair texture
My career
My status

Well today I speak on behalf of my dead brothers and sisters
And we want to know Why?

When daddy's sperm met with your seed
That was actually a miracle
To inform you of a blessing
So many still cry for
To remind you that sex
Is more than a game

We were supposed to receive the overflow
Of the love that you share
But you couldn't hear
The number of times we sent messages of love and gratitude
through the life-line
You didn't care that we felt every jab and stab before eventually
losing the life that we had
So today I hope you hear me, us
Why?

I HAVE A VOICE

(Trisha Leander)

I have a Voice
I don't think y'all heard me
So let me raise my volume
I have a Voice

I have a Voice
I ain't no ox so don't muzzle me
I live in a democracy where I am free
To express
So don't suppress me
I have a Voice

I have a Voice for Christianity
So if I choose to be moved by the Holy
Ghost
Who are you to judge me
I do not wish for you to define me
But to accept my purpose and the destiny
That my Father has predestined for me
To be the me that I was created to be
And not boxed in by someone else's
creativity
Or interpretation of the Word
When God has spoken to me
Because really and truly
Too fearful you are to stand up and stand
out

So you sit in and sit it out
Too comfortable to walk out in faith
So you get dressed and wait for ushers to
pass the plate
And go home to negotiate

Well I have a Voice
For every one of you
My sister and my brother
Massa days are over
We are not slaves to someone else's desire
To someone else's disaster
To fit in someone else's mold
And be told, or sold out
Where is your Voice
Your power
Your drive
Your ambition
Your talk
Your fire
Your prescription
To help you get over
Cross over
To get you to the other side
When are you gonna stop hiding
Behind someone else's Voice
You have a choice
You have a Voice

I have a Voice for Tobago
Sweet Tobago, the land of my birth
One of the blessed countries here on this
earth
So what, I represent the 10% of
Tobagonians
Who decided to stay here
But I fail to represent this 10% of
Tobagonians
Who decide to stay here
I don't think y'all heard me
So I say again
I represent the 10% of Tobagonians
Who decided to stay here
But I fail to represent this 10% of
Tobagonians
Who decide to stay here
Stay in my mind of waiting for someone
else to tell me
That my island is unique and filled with
endless treasures and beauty
That my eyes are too long to see what I
have right here in front of me
Because I continue to compare myself
with other countries
So then I become a wannabe
So what? Doesn't Tobago have a sense of
identity
To create for itself what can occur
naturally

Doesn't Tobago have a Voice of its own
Tobago has a choice to discern its own
Path, Destiny, how best to utilize its
resources
Which of course are incomparable
To what any other country owns
So when are we gonna put down the
senseless pride and jealousy and anger
and all the negativity
And develop a greater sense of 'ah we' and
unity to endeavour to become a country
that has a vision to preserve our integrity
Don't sit by idly while the authorities
make decisions that fill their pockets
with treasures like citizen pirates of this
economy
Don't you know that the state of this state
lies in the Voice of people like you and me

Well I have a Voice
For every one of you
My sister and my brother
Massa days are over
We are not slaves to someone else's desire
To someone else's disaster.
Like Martin Luther
Don't you have a dream?
Don't sit there like Rosa Parks
Because she sat for a cause
To break the laws

That opened doors that no longer exist
So we can walk anywhere
Despite our colour
Where are the Nelson Mandelas of this
era
Mahatma Gandhis
While we sit idly by as our youths are
being devoured
Slipping through the cracks
While their cracks are being exposed
More tattoo marks on their bodies
Than any mark they would make in this
part of the world
Already indoctrinated by the previous
'Gaza and Gully' code
Why not, when the media hits them up
like crack on a high just so that they could
remain low
Who cares what Vybes Cartel is on
Why should I have my mind infiltrated by
another country's culture and delinquents
Chanting disrespect and curse words
More like curses on your daughters and
sons
So don't cry when our youths bring us
shame
Washing the works of our ancestors down
the drain
No work ethics, after they worked so hard
to build this island

No customer care orientation, poor
service mentalities, not to mention
This cell phone and technology
generation
Face it, Facebook should issue a degree
To every one
For spending all their free time online
And reducing this nation's level of
production
While our students utilize their free
computers for pornography, cyber
bullying and playing games like a Play
Station
Leading themselves to the path of
destruction
The future of this nation, wooooooooo
Why not, as parents maybe I should
prescribe some Buckley's or Chandelier
Bush
Because you have no Voice
Never at home, poor children are always
left alone
Too busy making money, making a lime,
enjoying your time
Studying, working, liming, sleeping
Sleeping, that's what you are doing
So blame it on the fact that father left
you, or the mother
Blame their failure on every teacher

Blame the pregnancy and delinquency on
a neighbour or stranger
Then blame the state of this country on
the church or the Prime Minister
Do you have a Voice for Tobago
Do you have a Voice at all
Well I have a Voice
One that must be heard
Not just to do Spoken Word
Action speaks louder than words
Father, promote me
My resume´ must never read hypocrite
I must not just be defined by 'Literate'
You see out of the abundance of my heart
My mouth speaketh
Out of the desires of God's heart
I now liveth
So let today mark my indignation
Let this world know I tender my
resignation
For this is the appointed hour
That this world realizes who I am
I am Trisha Leander
No entertainer
But this world's needed change-maker
Hallelujah!

$\mathcal{H}$andel Dillon

Handel Dillon is a retired secondary school teacher. He taught at Bishop's High School for 35 years and retired as head of the Physical Department of that school. His official specialty is Integrated Science and Physical Exercise however Handel Dillon is recognized as one of the best exponents of the oral traditions of Tobago. He is a master at the art of creating old time Tobago wedding speeches and eulogies. Handel is married

OLE TIME TOBAGO WEDDING SPEECH
On behalf of the Bride
By *Handel Dillon*

Honourable ladies and honourable gentleman dem. Dis momentous occasion fills my heart with philanthropic gratification and jubilation!

As I examinate the physiognomy of all dem preposterous damsels and jezebels present here in their exquisite paraphernalia, I experience a sensation of verbal constipation. Nevertheless, the forces of necessity have compelled me to explatiate on the Words of the Psalmist David – "Behold! How good and how pleasant it is for brethren to dwell together in unity."

Officially ascribed with the portfolio of designated Godfather, it is my distinguished desire to propose a toast to the bride. I personally had the distinct pleasure and privilege of clinically supervising this pertinaciously precious specimen of human anatomy from the bud to dis holistic entity - voluptuous, aesthetically pleasing and properly laminated.

And so, as I contemplate on what I am about to ejaculate, I stand predominate when I categorically declare that by no stretch of the imagination can anyone point a finger in Jestina face because of her perspicatiousness. For when coming to cook, she is a proficient kitchen mechanic; when coming to wash and keep house, she is highly qualified; and when coming to hold and keep ah man, she is competently endowed with the capacity to cling tenaciously to any long-suffering victim of pusillanimous circumstances.

Yes indeed, Mr. Bridegroom, you have a prized possession. It is therefore incumbent that your credentials are up to mark to contend with this insatiable, hot-blooded thorough-bred. Notwithstanding that you are now a licensed practitioner, your performance will determine your destiny. With testicular fortitude, be ready like Freddy cause she has acrobatic propensity.

And now that this nuptial union has reached the desired climax, you must discharge you responsibility by proceeding most impregnatiously with the developmental programme. It is imperative and logical to conclude. Do not be overwhelmed with orgasmic exuberance because anxiety paralyses activity. Mr. Gentleman, I wish you a smooth take-off and a happy landing.

As the two of you both are now vested with the official dispensation to be fruitful and multiply, procreation must follow celebration.

And before I terminate my synopsis and extricate myself from this predicament, I want to simultaneously thank you the guesses from the bottom of my diaphragm for your profusely explicit constitution and tolerance. Eat, drink and be merry for the harvest is plenteous but the labourers are few.

Permit me momentarily to advance my strategic position of perpetual cohabitation compatible with a successful consummation.

Cheers! Thank You.

© Handel Dillon

$\mathscr{C}$rystal Skeete

Crystal G. Skeete grew up in a single-parent-extended family household as the youngest and only female among her siblings. This 28 year old Tobagonian attended Bishop's High School from 1998 to 2005 and later became the recipient of the John Streetly Memorial Scholarship fund and a Further Additional National Scholarship. She went on to pursue medicine at the University of the West Indies' (UWI) St. Augustine Campus where she attained a Bachelor in Medical Sciences in 2011 and a Bachelor in Medicine, Bachelor in Surgery (MBBS) in 2013.

In addition to her scholastic endeavours a love for literature has always been a part of her life and she has found an avenue for expression through spoken word poetry. This poet holds the title of 2013 Verses Bocas Literature Festival Poetry Slam as well as the 2014 Tobago Word Festival Speak and Compete Poetry Slam champion. She has partnered with the 2 cents movement as well as the Free Speech Project to share several pieces of her work; the most popular to date being "*Maxi Man Tracking School Gyal.*" Unlike her grandmother's generation she believes that young ladies must be seen as well as heard and so uses spoken word as a tool to express her truth on relevant issues.

Life in 'Bago

By Crystal G. Skeete

I am a proud Tobago Trini!
Yes!!
Take one good look at me and you will see that this is what a
proud West Indian looks like
But this is also what a proud Tobagonian looks like!
My Trini friends tell me they does know I from Tobago because
of my accent and the extra 'Tobago glow' on my nose,
That makes me an expert on life in Bago I suppose,
My navel string buried in Buccoo beneath a buck buck tree,
The same tree my grandfather used to fertilize with pee when
it needed salts.

Yuh see,
I didn't have the modern nuclear family I grew up with the
extended,
Which meant that cultures and traditions extended way
beyond the generational gap,
So I used to sit with the elders and listen to them talk about
the old time days,
We used to reminisce about their *old time ways,*
And then we would wish to *bring it back bring it back.*
So I know what it is to go market and get lagniappe,
Or be rude and get a good slap from yuh aunty and then a
next one when she decide to tell yuh mammy,

I had a good taste of Tobago and it wasn't just the blue food,

I learned not to be rude because *laugh and cry live in the same house,*
A statement my granny used to preach,
And I will not forget the things my granny used to teach,
So I will *never hang mih hat where mih hand cyar reach.*
This *cockroach never dance in fowl party,*
I learn to be independent cuz *every pot have to stand up on its own bottom,*
Still I appreciate that *no one man is an island,*
And that is exactly why I love my island,
We know 'bout lend hand, we does come together to throw sou sou,
We doh protest and burn tyre we content to sousou sousou,
Generally we prefer to live life under the radar,
So the neighbours will cuss out but they hardly ever fight,
We win wars with we mouth not with guns and knife,
But be prepared to get cuss bout yuh brother, nenen, tantie, cousin and father,
Like Jack Warner we will cuss yuh bout yuh mudda,

We will call yuh locho, zantipweh, bebe and obzokie,
We will say yuh wife have yuh tutulbay like yuh need licks with red panty,
We will talk 'bout yuh eye whether it big or cokey,
We will describe yuh foot whether it K or bandee,
We would kill yuh with picong and mek yuh get laugh from everybody,
And then when we done is back to full unity,
Wedding, christening or wake we up and ready cuz ultimately,
All ah we is one family.

And speaking bout family,

I swear we is the only island where people does come from any land and ask for the tall, red man who does drive the old, blue van and expect yuh to know exactly who it is.

I doh know 'bout you but I fed up of the random stranger quiz!

The 'Aye you from Tobago?'

Yeah.

'Which part?'

Les Coteaux.

'Or suh that mean yuh know a fella name Boongie? He from somewhere up Roxborough...........'

Seriously!!!

Ah mean the island small but I doh literally know everybody!

But yuh know the part that does get to me?

Is the fact that half the time Boongie does turn out to be mih family.

On another note,

You ever bounce up on a good outside lime,

With fire wood and coconut shell and 3-stone fire side?

Where everybody bring what dey have and put it in a pool,

Then is oil-down, yabba, buljol and peas soup; thing to mek yuh drool,

Rehl people does show up to eat but it only had 3 cook,

But dais what we like .... just take a look at we fuh harvest,

Taking loan from Republic to make each year happen better than the rest,

Doh talk 'bout Buccoo Goat Race fuh Easter, we put a mountain on yuh plate,

We feed people we don't know and everybody get a taste
Because in Tobago is better belly buss than good food waste.

Ah wouldn't be complete talking 'bout life in Tobago if ah
didn't tell yuh bout a little thing we have that some call macco,
Tallpree came close when he say everybody peeping,
But we doh peep we does watch cuz is we neighbour back we
keeping,
Comess is the island-wide language that everybody could
understand,
Is always he say that she say that somebody tek yuh man,
I doh call it comess, I does call it history,
Cuz we talking 'bout things that happen already,
It is past tense and just a narration of events,
It becomes comess when you try to change the sequence,
So people does dey lockup tight tight in dey house,
And know whether yuh mekking left hand dumpling or chicken
foot souse,
Dey know who is yuh chile fadda before you get pregnant,
And if yuh put them in they place they know how yuh
ignorant,
Shopkeeper does know all who ah tek man and who throw
away baby,
But she cyar see when she own business running way from she,
Business left Mt. St George gully and deh ah Les Coteaux
hilltop,
Still dat cyar mek she mouth shut up,
Tuck shop tun talk shop,
Paul Keens tun up!

Like fowl cock she a crow mekkin announcement every morning,
She tek way George Leacock wuk she is the village Tambrin.
Acquiring second hand information like a passive smoker,
The Tobago village macco ain't no joke nah!

All in all
This island is one that have plenty vibe,
Is only a matter of time before the news reach worldwide,
But when in Tobago do as the Tobagonians do,
Keep the island Clean, Green, Safe and Serene,
So that she will *become more beautiful*,
And life in Tobago will always be full…

Vernon Aqui

1955 - 2015

Science Educator in Tobago and the Caribbean. Author of science texts, stories and poems. And so much more.

Quote:
"I did what I came here to do"

It is the author's hope that his stories and poems would inspire others to do
'What they came here to do.'

A Youth Man's Prayer

God loves a nice thing,
Only touch my bling and you'll feel 'cheerful giver',
Give me all you've got,
Your rings, your purse, yuh gold chain too,
Just give to me the whole damned lot.
Don't do hard work but like my sting.
Can't sleep at night, plenty work put down,
With gun and knife I'll track yuh down.
I'll shoot yuh wife, yuh child, de dog,
To show you boy, that man done past.
De blue light shine, youth man, best run fast,
The Babylon come, they'll kill meh ass.
With bullet and gun, no way to pass,
Meh back ah bun, I did hear the gun.
Everything get dim, ah go die in sin?
Meh partners run, ah fall to the ground,
Forgive me Lord for the things I've done.
It's never too late to find yuh pearly gate.
The time is right, so please, why wait?
Ah go just say, "Forgive me Lord."

Oh how I love Thee Lord

I rise from my bed each day,
And say good morning God.
He answers with the oh
sweet song,
From everything around.

I see him in the fish that
swim,
Butterflies, bees, birds and
trees.
His wondrous works he
made to show,
To us who do believe.

Oh how I love this mighty
God,
Who fills my heart with awe,
I'll love and shout and praise
his name,
His mercy to endure.

All honour I give to you Oh
Lord,
Your works remain
unchanged,
Through faith, and hope His
mighty name,
I always will proclaim.

Oh how I love you precious
God,
On you my life depends.
You gave Your Son who died
for us,
To wash away our sins.
His precious blood we all
saw spill,
The scourging he took for
me,
They saved me from the grip
of sin
So I'll live forever more.

On the ground was shed that
blood,
Those stripes which he
received,
The falls he bore, the nails
that tore,
Too much, we couldn't
endure.

On the cross that fateful day,
He hung for all to see,
The spear they thrust into
His side,
He died for you and me.

I don't deserve your suffering
Lord,
Your love, it knows no
bounds.

With full breath from within
my chest,
I shout 'How Great Thou
Art'.

Isabel Turner-Toby

ISABEL TURNER-TOBY was born in Tobago and has been a primary school teacher for the past fourteen (14) years. She is married with one daughter.

Isabel is a graduate of both the University of the West Indies and the University of Michigan from which institutions she holds, respectively, a Bachelor's Degree in Psychology and Sociology and a Master's degree in Education.

Isabel began writing in 2004 while participating in a course – The Teaching of Reading. Although she has written several books and poems, she is yet to publish any.

When she is not teaching, she is travelling, reading, communicating or painting faces. She also loves spending time outdoors, planting in her garden with her daughter, Shenequa.

Shenequa's Secret

"Mummy, Mummy, where are you?" asked an assertive voice. Mummy smiled because that was the voice of her daughter, Shenequa Toby.

'I am here, baby," she answered back. "I'm in the kitchen."

"Ooh," was the only response she heard before she saw her cute, round face appearing in the kitchen.

"Mummy, where is my daddy?" she asked.

"He is at work, Shenequa," her mother replied.

"I want to see my daddy," came a sharp reply. "When is my daddy coming home?"

"Is he bringing my puppy for me?" she continued.

"Puppy, puppy, ruff, ruff," said her little brother Shaughn.

"Shenequa! We said no."

"Please Mummy, pl-e-a-s-e," she begged in a soft, sweet voice. But to no avail.

"You can't take care of a puppy, my dear. When you are older we will get you one. Ok, baby?"

"Ok Mummy," she answered in a soft, disappointed voice, and turned and walked away.

Unknown to her parents, Shenequa had been promised a dog by a family friend, Jade. That very evening, while sitting and having a snack after playing with Jade in the park near her home, Shenequa enquired about the puppy. She told Jade that she would take the puppy, but wants it kept a secret.

"But Shenequa," questioned Jade, "how would you keep a puppy a secret from your parents? Wouldn't they find out? Where would you keep the dog?"

"I don't know, but I will find a place in my bedroom to keep him safe."

That evening, while her mother was on the computer and her dad was washing the car, Shenequa collected the puppy. Hiding under her jersey was a small puppy, whimpering under its master's clothes. He was the cutest puppy she ever saw, a mixture of Cavalier and Chihuahua, with white fur and a pair of loving brown, trusting eyes.

The next week passed without incident. Shenequa had her puppy and her parents were still unaware of the visitor in her room. Daily she would save scraps from her breakfast, lunch and dinner for her pet. An old bowl from the kitchen was its feeding dish.

At evening, Shenequa hastily finished her dinner to retreat to the safety of her room where she could play with Spot. He was everything she wanted in a puppy. He was playful, loyal and friendly. His tail was always wagging as she entered the room. He slept under her bed dutifully every night and greeted her each morning with licks and kisses.

However, one morning, while at the breakfast table, her mom complained that the left side of her slippers had gone missing. She enquired of all, "Has anyone seen my slipper?" Both her husband and her daughter denied seeing it.

"Hey, maybe you left it somewhere else. You will find it later, I'm sure," her husband replied.

"Yes, I'm sure I will," agreed Shenequa's mother.

But for the next two weeks, things continued to go missing. Her father couldn't find a side of one of his shoes and one of his favourite slippers.

"Something is wrong here. I can't seem to find the blue towel that was hanging on the rail.

Yesterday, the mat was torn to pieces. On Wednesday, the bread on the table had bites on it. I had to throw it all away. What is going on here? It seems that things are just disappearing. Is it you Shenequa or is it Shaughn? Were you the one who bit the bread on the table?"

"No, Mummy, I did not touch it. It's not me," she said.

"No, not me!" repeated her little son, shaking his head.

"Ok baby, but something is just not right."

'Maybe it's the neighbour's dog. I am almost certain it comes over when we are not at home and removes things," her mother continued as she tried to solve the mystery.

"Yes Mom, that's true. You remember last Christmas you had us search all over the house for the decorations? You thought that they were stolen from the tool shed. But later we found them under the water tank. Remember we blamed the boy, Johnny, next door? You even said that Aunt Jenny threw them away. Remember?"

"Oh my," exclaimed her mother. "I will look for them."

That night, after everyone had gone to sleep, Shenequa lay in bed, concerned. She kept wondering if somehow Spot was responsible for any of the items that were missing. How was it that things were missing from the house? The bread was bitten. Dad's slippers and shoes had been left inside. Maybe, these things were just misplaced and would be found later.

"Spot, did you leave this room when I was out during the day?"

"Ruff, ruff," was the only reply that came from the puppy as he started to lick Shenequa's face, indicating that he was ready to play. She was so sure that it wasn't her puppy that she immediately removed the thought from her mind and went to play merrily with her pet.

It was Easter Sunday and Shenequa's cousin, Jade came over. They were all going to an Easter Sunday Service at the Montgomery church. Everyone was in their room getting dressed when Jade came knocking on her aunt's door. "Aunty Belle, Aunty Belle, where are you? What shoes is Shenequa going to wear? She doesn't know what to wear."

"Yes, Shenequa, yes. Wear the pink shoes with that dress. Okay, baby?"

"Ok Aunty,' she said, and was off to Shenequa's room.

"In a few minutes Shenequa was shouting to her mother. "Mummy, I can't find my pink shoes. We looked everywhere. I don't know where it is. Shaughn maybe moved it."

"Ok Shenequa, I will come and look for it for you. They are your shoes. You should be able to find things there. I am sure both of you are not taking your time to look for them."

"No Mummy, we were looking for a very long time and we still can't find them."

"Come, we'll find them together," said her mother.

Shenequa and her mother headed for her room to look for her pink shoes. First her mother looked under her bed, but they weren't there. As she was lifting her head from under the bed she heard "Ruff, ruff."

Surprised by the strange noise, she hit her head against the edge of the bed in her haste to see what had made that sound. "Ouch! I hit my head. Did you hear that Shenequa? What was that sound?"

"Ooh!" was the only response that came from Jade.

"Ahm, what sound, Mummy?" Shenequa asked with a worried expression on her face.

But before her mom could repeat the question, the sound came again, "ruff ruff" coming from the region of the bath. "That sound!" her mother cried out, "Don't tell me you didn't hear it. It's coming from the bath tub."

At that moment, Shenequa's mom got up and raced to Shenequa's bath. On opening the bath room, what she saw surprised her. Inside the bath, was a white furry animal, chewing on one of Shenequa's pink shoes.

"Shenequa, SHENEQUA TOBY, come in here now!" shouted her mother, in an angry voice.

"Yes Mom." Shenequa answered, cautiously.

"What is that? Is that a puppy I see there eating your pink shoe?"

"My pink shoe?" mimicked Shenequa, in fear.

"Yes, chewing your pink shoe, in YOUR bathroom, in YOUR room. How did that puppy get inside here?" her mother asked with a strange expression on her face. "Shenequa, whose puppy is this?"

"It's my puppy, Mommy," Shenequa said in a defeated voice. "I always wanted a puppy but both you and Dad said I couldn't have one because I wasn't old enough and responsible enough."

"What!" exclaimed her mother in an angry voice. "Yes and ...?"

"W-e-l-l, Mom, I thought that if I got a puppy and took care of it, I could show you and Dad how good I was at taking care of it and you would let me keep him."

"But we said no, Shenequa, you disobeyed us. So wait, WAIT, this is the ONE that had taken my red slipper, your father's shoe and eaten the floor mat upstairs!"

"Yes Mom, I guess so! But mom I just wanted to show you that I can take care of him. Mom I love him. He keeps my company. He sleeps right here below my bed every night and licks my face every morning. Mom he loves me too. Please, Mom, please. Can I keep him? Please? I will clean up after him; I will bathe and take care of him. You will see. You and Dad wouldn't have to do a thing for him. Mummy, Spot," Shenequa said, pointing at her puppy, "is my best friend, my very best friend. Please Mummy." Shenequa begged her mother. At that moment, Spot came to Shenequa's mother's foot, rubbing his head against her leg, whimpering, as if he too were begging.

After hearing her daughter's pleas and the crying sound from the puppy, Shenequa's mom's heart was softened.

"Ok, ok, don't think that you can outsmart me. Ok, you can keep him, BUT," she paused, "you have to pay for the damages done by YOUR pet, Smot, Spot, whatever his name is."

"Ok Mummy," Shenequa said in a quiet voice, her eyes beaming with hope.

"You will scrub the baths in this house until you pay off for the damage done by YOUR pet. You will be paid a dollar for each room. All the money you will earn will go towards replacing the items Spot destroyed. Is that clear? You are to ensure that Spot is kept away from destroying anything else in this house. Ask your father to build a kennel for him and keep him out of your room. He is not to come upstairs. Do you hear me young lady?" Shenequa's mother asked.

"Yes Mummy, I do and I will keep him out. He will be the best puppy ever. You will see! Thank you Mummy," Shenequa said, as she hugged her mother tight.

"Don't commit wrong and think for a moment that you will escape. Remember the Bible says, '… be sure your sin will find you out'. Always be honest with your father, me and yourself."

"Yes, I understand," said Shenequa. She was very relieved; she got to keep her puppy. The punishment of cleaning all the bathrooms in the house was small in comparison to her gain. She no longer had to hide to play with her pet. Now Spot could play in the yard,

She could show him to all her friends and teach him lots of tricks. She was indeed fortunate to have her pet, Spot, but she did learn one thing…

'… *be sure your sin will find you out*'.

And her sin really did find her out.

The World Today

Today another young man is
dead
That's the news on the daily
head
Everyday another son is gone
Every day, another mother
bemoans
Alone in her fears, alone in
her tears
Who knows what she really
fears.
Every day is a murder,
thieving or raping
All seem lost, hopeless and
disbelieving
When will it all come to an
end?
Is it that we've all gone mad?
When did it all get so
horribly bad?
Where's the loving and care
we once had?
Will the madness and
lawlessness ever stop?
All this hating and killing
even by cops
Respect for life is a thing of
the past

Day after day, it's depleting
fast
Politician and preacher have
all lost their way
Hatred and anger, turmoil
and grief, is the way
Somebody let that handsome
devil loose
Who opens hell's door and
releases his noose
Damnation and hell, we're
living each day
Who said that this ought to
be the way?
The fires of hell and hatred
are burning bright
The smoke of despair like a
hovering light
Every institution in the
world is getting worse
Politician and professional
are working only for their
personal purse.
In recent years
corporal punishment
has ceased to exist
But not for teachers, they
now getting licks

Television, video
games, not mothers,
raising their child
But discipline those children
and the same mothers gone
wild
Who can blame the children
of today?
After all, they're looking to
find their own way.
Look in the court,
that's where the young
leaders are,
Error after error they're
doomed to make.
Everybody needs to work,
none can stand idly by
To restore the love, peace
respect, we all must try
With God Almighty we are
all in this together
Each one of us, our brother's
keeper.

MY LIFE

Born in Moriah in August, out of fornication
Life for me offered struggle and frustration.
Hence, education and hard work became my dedication
In order to survive and become someone of recognition.

Day after day, I give of my love and devotion
To the children of this blessed nation.
But life is strange and filled with provocation,
Without God, there will be no promotion.
Daily, I pray for blessing and protection
For my daughter and me, living with this challenging
generation.

My life is all about learning and gaining more education
In order to bring up my child in God's guidance and
benediction.
Life takes love, purpose and God's sanction
In order to become content and full of jubilation.
Fulfilling His works and His revelation
Is the purpose of my creation.

$\mathcal{J}$illian E. Moore

JILLIAN E. MOORE is a daughter of the Caribbean Soil - Tobago & Trinidad. She possesses a passionate interest in the Caribbean, its culture and its people. She has been a stalwart in the Metropolitan Caribbean Community mainly in Washington D.C, for the past thirty plus years. During these years Jillian has been involved in numerous Caribbean activities such as President of Juniors Soccer Club, President and Founder of Helping Hands of the Caribbean, (HHOTC), and Asphalt Productions.

Jillian has a passion for authentic calypsos and the rich cultural heritage for Trinidad and Tobago and the Caribbean generally. In her various capacities, Jillian has organized and hosted several Calypso extravaganzas and steelband concerts in the United States

Jillian is a volunteer Instructor of Community of Hope. Jillian enjoys painting and writing poetry, short plays, skits and monologues – about her formative years while growing up in Tobago and Trinidad. Her stage name is Keturia.

She's a storyteller/folklorist, an actress, a motivational speaker and a comedian/stand-up at open mike venues, churches and schools in North America and Canada. Jillian enjoys sharing her

W's viz: words of comfort, warm wishes, words of inspiration and words of wisdom. She always hopes that through her spiritual writings, her poems, short stories, or skits she can shed some sunshine and comfort on a lonely heart.

My Crystal Ball
(Jillian E. Moore)

Forgive me! But I did not comprehend
I said "Fifty Years."
OK! That's good
Now tell me what mark did you leave in the sand?

I can see how enthused you are, that's great but say what!
In my observation, I have not seen "Progress" of the "People"
However, I see cell phones of all descriptions and models
I see young men pants falling down from off their waistlines
I see young ladies, even mature women scarcely clad

I see Fast food restaurants popping up all over the Island
I see School Children without manners and respect for their
elders
I see "Doubles Stands" early on mornings to serve Breakfast
to School Children
I see on Sunday mornings empty Pews and the Elderly
I see men and women on the pulpit, but I can't see Ministers

I see filthy streets
I see beautiful Beaches competing with Trash for space
I see beautiful erected governmental buildings with uncouth
employees
I see fleets of vehicles travelling F A S T on our highways &
streets

I see Teachers not teaching and not respecting themselves
I see DRUGS taking over the bodies of our YOUTH
I see luscious fields but no livestock grazing
I see agricultural lands but nothing to harvest
I see TV programs with no substance to elevate the LEADERS
OF TOMORROW
I see CRIME as a Style
I see we are still enslaved but I can't see the broken shackles
I see politicians who are afraid to be honest with the masses
I see dishonest Police Officers

I see houses but I can't see homes
I see Children making Children but I can't see Parents
I see Sand, Sea & Bikinis but I can't see any African Queens
I see Students dying for Knowledge but I can't see a Library

I see you present for the quest for Knowledge but I can't see
what you will plant after leaving this Venue
Therefore, I charge you All to embrace at least three YOUTHS
and NURTURE them for the Future
I see your Trainees running the RACE for the next FIFTIETH
Jubilee
I see a CHANGE taking shape
Now tell me, what do you see?

$\mathcal{S}$harde Titus

SHARDE TITUS has been regularly described as 'artsy' due to the fact that she is always finding a way to do something creative. She has attained a degree in Literatures in English with a minor in theatre. She has also pursued a CVQ in television and video production Level 1 and currently pursuing level 2. She enjoys writing poetry, shorts stories and film scripts and has also been involved in a few projects making short films. She is passionate about finding a voice for women in her generation that can resonate with many in the Caribbean Region and the wider diaspora.

After having the privilege of living in three different islands in the Caribbean, Sharde has a wealth of stories waiting to be told. With these stories she hopes to highlight the beauty and the not so beautiful side of Caribbean people and the ebb and flow that makes us want to run but keep us staying on the islands as we would not want things to be any other way. While short stories are the beginning she dreams of working on a book that she describes as Harry Potter/Twilight/Grimm meets Caribbean folklore, and who knows this might become a reality.

SHE IS PEOPLE TOO!
(Sharde Titus)

"And the winner"…wasn't me, another year and I lost 'Steups'. Like my winning streak gone. Fifteen years I have been entering the midnight robber competition and I used to win. I used to win or come in the top three at least. I heard a rumour that I came third to last the only people I could beat was the fat guy who forgot his lines and the drunkard who entered every year in the same dirty smelly costume and said the same rhyme year after year. I was tired but I had to walk all the way to city gate in my costume, I felt sweaty underneath all that satin and cloth so I took off my robe and my top, leaving on my vest and my pants. I thought to myself that it's a good thing the evening sun was low, far beyond the horizon. I tried to avoid a small Maxi with my costume and my hat in my hand.

Out of all the seats she came and sat next to me and she looked like the leader of a big women band. Every minute she shifted around like I was not giving her enough space. A tight red vest and red leggings with holes down the side. It would have been nice to look at if she was slim or even thick and firm but she was not. The top she had on struggled to cover as much of her body as the fabric could stretch over. The driver did not waste time in collecting his money he wanted his money before he left the terminal. As he collected the six dollar fare his eyes roved looking hard at passengers with food in their laps. At the front of the maxi hung a crude sign that read; NO EATING, DRINKING OR SMOKING. SINCE YUH MOTHER LEAVE ME I HAVE NO ONE TO CLEAN!!

As he came down the aisle I started searching for my money. I found four dollars and kept searching for more but only found twenty five cents. I never walk with my wallet when I know I am going to perform as I always want the clothes to lie smoothly, but I thought I saved enough to go home clearly I wasted a thought. He saw me searching, and as he got closer and closer his indifferent expression changed to exasperation. "Yuh cum een meh maxi and yuh know yuh eh have the money. Allyuh always full of tricks. Allyuh feel I does get free gyas or something? Eh? Yuh feel my maxi running on oxygen? Come out, man! Big man like you and yuh tryin to play trick. MAN, PELT YUH TAIL OUT MIH MAXI!"

The fat lady next to me laughed as I began to hustle out of the maxi - a scandalous, raucous, loud laugh that attracted all the passengers' attention to the situation. Before I could move the driver took her six dollars and asked her if she was not paying for two seats. Startled by his question the lady stopped laughing abruptly and glared at him in disbelief and anger. Her eyes widened as she asked him to repeat himself. He leaned in a little closer and did just that "Miss lady, yuh can't make other passengers uncomfortable. Yuh need to pay fuh two seats or come out meh maxi, any way allyuh big women does mash up meh shocks!"

I slowed my pace out of the maxi as I tried to hear the conversation and look at the woman's reaction. I did not know if she would cry or curse but she chose the latter and began to wrap the driver like channa in barra with curse words. She spewed at him venomously, she told him about his old bus, about his ugly face that matched his ugly ways his mother was also thrown in there somewhere. The maxi driver now feeling low and embarrassed began hurling words back at her while walking off and he demanded that she took her heavy carcass off his maxi. I laughed as I tried to get off the maxi before the driver and I continued to look on at the incident from outside.

The lady started coming off the vehicle but before she left she remembered that she paid him. This began another argument as he insisted that he did not take her money. She stood in the middle of the maxi refusing to disembark quarrelling at the top of her voice. He now in the driver's seat began to drive off with her standing causing her to topple and fall. This irritated one of the women who was sitting next to her, she stood up and let the driver know between a flurry of obscene that he did take the money and should pay the woman back. She also told him she would report him for what he had said to the woman and for reckless driving. "Being fat is not a crime," she said. "The woman is people too! You insult the woman in yuh maxi and we women not standing for that nonsense." She pulled out her cell phone and dialed a number.

Feeling embarrassed he mumbled something under his breath and threw the six dollars in singles out the window and told her to go fetch. Before I could blink twice the transit police boarded the maxi and tried to stop the woman from hitting the driver anymore with her handbag. They pulled her off gave her six dollars from the driver and sent the driver out of the terminal after asking all his passengers to disembark. The whole situation made me forget about the hot day and the sweltering heat that my clothes was generating.

I found a pay phone and called my wife. She said my misfortune was an act of God as God always punishes those that take part in the devil's revelry. I waited for her outside the terminal and kept s short distance away from the fat lady who was now relating her version of the story to a man who appeared to be smitten with all her figure. I really felt sorry about how the maxi driver – and I too - had stereotyped her because of her size. Then I thought why she did not take care of herself better – or do like my wife and avoid the devil's revelry.

I did not get to complete this thought process as my wife arrived and stopped my trail of thought. As I got into the car I heard someone screaming my wife's name when I looked up I saw her coming towards the car. Her name was Annette. She went to primary school with my wife. I now knew her name and her history. Yes, she is somebody. She is people too – decent respectable people, my wife said to me.

$\mathscr{C}$hidimma Maynard

I am Chidimma Maynard, a full time single mom and creator of the Grace High Associative Learning Pre-School and founder of the first ever kids club in Tobago, Bounzy Children's Club. I have been in the pre-school business for the past four years and do enjoy teaching the young ones. Seeing them graduate, knowing that they have accomplished, brings me great joy.

In the past I have worked in different fields, one of them being in tourism where I worked as a front office operator at the Le Grand Courland & Grafton Beach Resort. I like meeting people, reading, exploring the outdoors, hiking, and writing. At present I am learning to play the keyboard and would like to excel, maybe even becoming an entertainer one day. At present, however, I am learning to play well so that I can teach the little students.

Motivational speaking is also one of my dreams as I have a natural ability to make others comfortable while listening to my ideas on different topics.

I'M NO HANDBAG
(From one woman to all important people.)

Handbags are usually good for USE
They come in every colour imaginable
They come in different shapes and sizes

We USE them to put our junk in
We USE them to put good things in too
Mostly we USE them to carry stuff around

People are not Handbags
Which we change to suite the occasion
They have feelings, desires and needs
People need only the good things in life
They have no need for junk
They have no need for stuff

We certainly don't need to be carried
Nor do we need to carry one another
We have feet for that
Mostly we can think
We can reason and we don't need to be USED
We can't be Handbags.

THE WICKED WOMAN

Why did she come?

To torture, to kill her own progeny.

Is it because of improper jealousy, one that should not be?

Is it because of greed, the avaricious type that never gets satisfied?

Is it hatred, the nastiest of the woes seen in her pretend-to-be-innocent eyes?

She is dark, as dark as night, her venom worse than a million cobra bites.

She sneaks up on her prey pretending non-intelligence. It is a lie!

One day she looks like you – human; the other – oh, what a fright, you can hardly believe the sight, you shudder, chills run down your spine.

You wonder at the instant metamorphosis as her next victim approaches, she turns again to light and feigns innocence, as she seeks to capture their ignorance. Her voice changes to that of a shuddering old woman in need of pity and help. Do not be fooled – RUN!

Her web is a hundred million times more tangled than the widow spider's.

She reels you in slowly, unsuspectingly. Those eyes deceitful, dreadful, lying always on the verge of tears. If you do not leave when they well up slightly, you too would be crying soon, if you survive her deadly venom.

Each attempt you make at kindness to her, is reeling you in for her kill. Like the praying mantis devours her mate while giving him intimacy.

She offers infinitesimal portions of kindness while flooding her victim with hate – the type that kills, so poisonous and disguised. You realize it one night when your heart is aching over the mismatched romance.

The pain from her bite is everlasting, going on and on if you are unsuspecting, because today it is healed to be opened again tomorrow with so much more agony.

Her attacks are constant not sporadic, and so slow you can never know. Do not love her she will hate you, she will hurt you in so many ways; a dictionary well written, could not describe such hurt.

Even many, many lifetimes put together cannot describe her. Like the Anaconda she consumes you whole crushing and squeezing you; she tangles you up masticating your bones in her inside.

Her other victims see no evidence of you, her last slaughter. A clean plate is always offered. It seems to be white. Look closer. It is off-white turning to grey. Do not look away. It is black. She is on the attack, don't turn your back. There is the hacker, her eyes as red as the darkest, deepest crimson rose turning to black.

Run, run, run! Do not look back. She has a beautiful profile, beautiful form, feigned grace, ladylike gait – only love and beauty could come from such a queen. Don't be fooled. She has many, many schemes.

Her piety and love for the divine can tie you up with so much fine twine; look away or you would be blind. When with her you can feel like the only lover that is until her other turns the corner.

You are scorned, spat out and rejected. All the good you did turns to excrement, in an instant, and you are an image, an apparition. Then her other unsuspecting victim becomes one himself and so it continues – her stream of assumed innocence, venomous love-hate, shameless disgust.

Harvey Anthony

Harvey Anthony is a prolific composer of poems short stories and most of all calypsoes. He specializes in humorous calypsoes with good clean lyrics. Harvey always has a story to tell. He is an exponent of the oral traditions of the Caribbean and likes to recount and record stories of the good old days.

THINK AGAIN
(Harvey Anthony)

All we DOING IS COMPLAINING
We not changing the way WE LIVING
We always think that GAMBLING
Is the only form of INVESTING
Morality and INTEGRITY
Are nowhere in our PSYCHE
To correct the only thing in USE
Is obscene and physical ABUSE
Idol worship in our RELIGION
We think will bring SALVATION
Segregation and Racial HATE
Would never make this country GREAT
When we start getting PROBLEM
We only blaming the SYSTEM
What Adults doing and SAYING
Is what children CULTIVATING
So starting from TODAY
Be example show the proper WAY
You cannot chart your DIRECTION
Before you know your DESTINATION
No one can lead from BEHIND
The blind cannot lead the BLIND
Let's hold hands and walk side by SIDE
In togetherness success will ABIDE

BUILDING A NATION
(Harvey Anthony)

I want to give my
DEFINITION
Of how we must grow as a
NATION
A Nation under God's LAW
Just As it was BEFORE
A nation of TOTAL UNITY
DISCIPLINE
TOLERANCE and
PRODUCTIVITY
Where every Creed and
RACE
Can find an equal PLACE
Let us be a Model Nation
In this Sunny Caribbean
Let us change the STATUS
QUO OF TRINBAGO
And go back as the way we
WERE

We sinking in the ABYSS of
DESTRUCTION
We on the path of TOTAL
DESOLATION
By discarding from the
NATION'S STRUCTURE

The Rule of Law and
ORDER
Every year there are
Hundreds of MURDERS
Bandits giving people
HORRORS
Let us stop Child –
ABORTION
And ABORT RAPE THEFT
and CORRUPTION
Let us build on the Nation's
PSYCHE
With the Pillars of
MORALITY
We must stop this IDOL
WORSHIP
Or SIN going to sink this
ship
The TRIPOD of this
NATION
Is DISCIPLINE
TOLERANCE and
PRODUCTION
Please don't tell a LIE
Is everyone getting an equal
share of the PIE

Is there equal
OPPORTUNITY
To citizens of this
COUNTRY
The Destitute and the Poor
in the DITCH
No help them getting from
the RICH
To get this nation back on
COURSE
Is to develop the Human
RESOURCE
Some, Living in ABJECT
POVERTY
That's not how it must BE

The way to build a
NATION
Is by making the right
DECISION

We must seek the advice of
the ALMIGHTY
By kneeling and praying
CHRISTIANITY
Those who we vote in
POWER
Must firstly obey Divine
ORDER
The way to grow as a
PEOPLE
Is to show the right
EXAMPLE
Only Time will TELL
If we going Up or Down the
WELL
Peace and Love is the
WATER
To put out this consuming
FIRE

A LESSON TO LEARN

(Harvey Anthony)

One must always REMEMBER
Experience is the greatest TEACHER
History relates the events of the PAST
The Future always comes LAST
The End – Result of your ACTION
Is what is called PREDESTINATION

There is a Role every human has to PLAY
The Script has been written that WAY
Obedience to Righteousness is a DIVINE LAW
Happiness is what we living for

CHORUS

In life there is always a lesson to LEARN
See listen and try to DISCERN
Try not to fall in the same HOLE AGAIN
It's a Prescription to avoid more PAIN

You dig a well to find WATER
Some wells are SHALLOW some are DEEPER
In the Dark you need a LIGHT
Not to stumble and fall in the NIGHT
So in a way you are preparing the FUTURE
To make life's journey SMOOTHER
Every letter must have a STAMP
In the same way you put oil in your LAMP
Preparation and Determination are Tools of Life's
TRADE
That is how the Future is MADE

Gloria Austin

GLORIA AUSTIN, born and raised in Tobago, is a retired administrative assistant who lived and worked in Canada for many years. She has written two self-published pocket books, "Beyond Appearances (When Things Go Wrong)" in 2002 and "Born For a Purpose" in 2003. She is also the editor of a newsletter, "The Labourer", a publication of the Bethesda Moravian Church Women's Fellowship.

"Heart to Heart" –
(One woman's personal experience with breast cancer)
[Excerpts from her soon-to-be published book, included
with her permission]
Gloria Austin

CHAPTER I

The Diagnosis

It is interesting that having passed my threescore years and ten and living on borrowed time biblically, my body was diagnosed with cancer of the breast in November 2011. Did this signal the end of my life? Read on.

The pundits tell us that we are all born with cancer cells. They are something to be feared for they create havoc within the body. Yet, the Psalmist praised God, our Maker, for the design of his body. "I will praise thee, for I am *fearfully and wonderfully made,"* (Psalms 13: 14) If we are fearfully and wonderfully made, why do we have cancer cells? What are their purposes? Does anyone know?

When the surgeon told me that the dis-ease in my body resulted in cancer, I did not react until he mentioned the word mastectomy to which I exclaimed, ***"What?"*** It never entered my mind to ask myself the question, ***"Why me?"*** for had I done so, I would have been pointing my finger at someone else. Why would I wish this dis-ease of the body on anyone when we are told to love our neighbour as ourselves?

Asking "why me" is not loving myself or my neighbour. Random acts do happen and *"time and chance happens to us all"*. These random acts and time and chance test our faith. James tells us that when we face trials (these random acts and time and chance) of any kind, to consider them nothing but pure joy because it is the testing of our faith which produces endurance. Though we would rather not have them, these random acts of time and chance enable us to bring out the best in us.

Since we are to be perfect therefore as our heavenly Father is perfect, when we experience suffering from things going wrong, we can use them to perfect us. From Jesus' suffering, he learnt obedience. *"Though he were a Son, yet learned he obedience by the things which he suffered, and being made perfect…"* (Hebrews 5; 8-9, KJV) Perfection is the state of being complete, finished, faultless. The state of being perfect results in love.

Not one of us is perfect; therefore, not one of us can go through life unscathed. But, when the challenges do come to better us and come they will, we each like to know that there is someone who can hold our hand. Look beyond the appearance of the challenge to the One who is waiting on the other side of the valley in which you find yourself, to the One who is willing and ready to help, and repeat these words *"Even though I walk through the darkest valley, I fear no evil, for you are with me, your rod and your staff, they comfort me"* (Psalms 23: 4, NRSV)

Jesus too suffered leaving us an example that we should follow in his steps. He could have asked ***"Why me?"*** because he committed no sin neither was deceit found in his mouth, but he did not. No one is exempt from pain and suffering no matter how hard we try, but we can use it to our advantage to bring out the best in us and to get to know ourselves.

Though I did not ask *"Why me?"* I did wonder what activated the cells. Whatever it is, it has opened my eyes like Job's to see how wonderfully and fearfully made I am and for this I give thanks. *"I have heard of thee by the hearing of the ear, but now mine eye seeth thee."* (Job 42: 5)

CHAPTER II

The Causes

There are different reasons given for the cause of cancer, some of which are exposure to chemicals in the environment, non-release of old hurts and resentments from the past which are referred to as cellular memories which saps our energy leaving us vulnerable, heredity, lifestyle choices, cells growing out of control, mold, lack of Vitamin D, low oxygen in the body's cells, lack of proper energy flow, excess estrogen in our food and water, mucus and in the case of breast cancer – underwire bra, iodine deficiency and on and on it continues as more discoveries are made.

Mucus

Cancer cells feed on mucus. Some foods like dairy products, wheat products, refined carbohydrates and dried foods cause mucus because of an allergic reaction to these foods.

Bacteria in the body can use sugar for food, thus weakening the immune system. Mucus is associated with the respiratory system, the gastrointestinal tract and the lymphatic system. Excess mucus creates a feeding ground for viruses.

The over-cooking of the oils and fats or trans-fat in fried foods stimulates the production of mucus. When we say *"I have a frog in my throat,"* I wonder if the frog is not mucus.

Raw fruits and vegetables are excellent mucus cleansers as they supply nutrients for healing, rejuvenation and the replacement of old cells with new ones.

These causes create a breakdown of the immune system. Cancer cells, present in our bodies are kept in control by a special immune cell, NK. When this is weak whether from old age, poor nutrition or stress, the cells multiply with nothing to hold them in check. Cancer cells supposedly thrive on solid foods but lots of people eat solid foods and do not have cancer, so what activates them in some and not in others?

There are so many different types of cancer – breast, prostate, lung, ovarian, mouth, throat, etc., etc. It seems as though there is one for every part of the body because these cells are everywhere and are not localized. Since my diagnosis is for breast cancer, I can write about that experience only though I will also be generalizing on cancer itself.

CHAPTER III

My Wonderfully Made Body

In my research into the disease, I was amazed at my discoveries, one of which was how fearfully and wonderfully made I am. Understanding how the body is made and the part it plays in its dis-ease can remove this fear of any dis-ease *"for God hath not given us the spirit of fear but of power and of love, and of a sound mind."* (11 Timothy 1: 7)

The body's cells have their own intelligence as they communicate with one another. They even change themselves into another type of cell if needed and know how to heal. Before an immune cell secretes any cancer-fighting agent, it has to identify the existence of cancer cells. It uses messengers called T-cells to notify the rest of the immune system to activate itself and produce cells to kill the cancer cells. The body tags the cancer cells to be destroyed, to prevent the killer cells from wiping out the wrong ones. How does the body know to do all this? *"...marvellous are thy works and that my soul knoweth right well."* (Psalms 139: 14)

Have you ever heard of apoptosis? It is the death of cells. This is the method the body uses to destroy these cells. Cells signal their own termination to keep the body's natural process of cell division in check. Those that are damaged or infected remove themselves from the body through apoptosis without harming other cells. The cells reduce in size and break down into fragments enclosed in membranes so as not to harm nearby cells.

The body heals itself. When we cut ourselves, the cut heals all by itself. Why can't the body heal itself of this malfunction – cancer? Is it that where the cut is concerned we do not think about it because we expect it to heal, that our mind is not involved or we take it for granted but where cancer is concerned, our mind is involved with fear of the disease, fear of death?

The word "cancer" puts fear into our hearts because we associate it with death but not so with Alzheimer, stroke or heart attacks. In days of yore, it used to be hush-hush as though just the mention of the word would make it contagious and shameful.

We create our fear of it but fear is an illusion which masks our power. *"For God hath not given us the spirit of fear but of power..."* (11 Timothy 1: 7) When He breathed His breath into us, it was the breath of life. Life is power not fear. Do not look upon cancer as a death sentence but as an opportunity to know your body which is *fearfully and wonderfully made*. We have the power to heal our bodies. Get past the emotion of fear.

We generate our fears. We do not create our fears only in the now but also into the future which is not even here now. Fear plagues us constantly, so we prepare ourselves for some disasters that might happen. When we fear, we worry. We fear because we have not yet entered that area of trust in the One who made us for His pleasure. Fear drives away all thought of not being given the *"spirit of fear but of power and of a sound mind."*

We make ourselves sick from worrying when we are afraid and without realizing it, our attitude of worrying is saying that the all-powerful God is not powerful enough to work out what we are afraid of. This is not true. He did not place the spirit of fear within us, we did that on our own. He gave us power, love and a sound mind. Our minds are not sound when we are fearful. Day and night we are obsessed by thoughts which enter our minds. This unsound mind is harmful to our health and peace of mind.

We have to surrender our fears before we can have the power, love and sound mind. We have to be unconcerned about the things we are fearful about knowing that everything is alright. Some of our fears do not make sense and need to be examined to find the root cause.

Apparently, our bodies have about 50 trillion cells with 1.17 volts of electricity in each cell. With knowledge of this much power in my body, why should I not believe that it is capable of healing itself?

CHAPTER IV

Thoughts

"For he that wavereth is like a wave of the sea driven with the wind and tossed for let not that man think that he shall receive any thing of the Lord. A double minded man is unstable in all his ways." (James 1: 6-8)

One has to be watchful over thoughts for they seem to have a mind of their own. Even though you think positively, the negative thoughts come creeping in. My sister who has passed her threescore years and ten (70) expects to be looked after because as she puts it, she is old. Since we live within a stone's throw of each other, it is her expectation that I look after her. There was a great temptation to not do all that I could to restore my health, to just give in by doing nothing so that I won't be a leaning post for her. She has no aches, pains or diseases, but since I am on spot, in her mind, I should be caring her.

The temptation was great to just give up for I saw her dependency on me as a burden which I did not need. Anger, bitterness and resentment are detrimental to our health and it was important that they be removed from my thoughts. I did not want to be "a double minded man" which would prevent me from receiving healing from my Creator.

When we have reached a certain age, we can become so self-centered that it leads to selfishness as we think the world revolves around us and no one else as we think: *"I have reached this age therefore I am entitled to do absolutely nothing, to not live my life and have someone else live it for me."* Fear of *"Who will help me now? Who can I run to now?"* has put her in a state of denial. Since her thoughts are not on me, I cannot count on her support. Realistically, we have to see people as they are and accept them as is, though painful.

Mention is made of my sister not to denigrate her by drawing attention to her but to show how I could have allowed her to influence my state of mind into giving up so that I won't have to deal with her.

CHAPTER V

Handling the Dis-ease

I was asked by the doctor if anyone in the family had cancer. Two cousins and an aunt died after being diagnosed with it. Was this my fate too? I chose not to believe it. I absolutely refuse to give cancer any power at all over me. It is not a good thing to inherit and I had no intention of doing so. It is important not to give the dis-ease a name. Giving the dis-ease of the body a name conjures up in the mind the stigma attached to it. Rather, think of it as a malfunction of the body. In thinking this way, your attitude will be to get the body functioning again. This removes the *"woe is me"* attitude and waiting passively for someone telling you what to do as you give your life over to others. Take action. Do your own research. What may work for one person may not work for you. Everyone's immune system is different.

Do not identity with the cancer. You are not it and it is not you. If you are not comfortable with conventional treatment, then research alternatives. One alternative is a diet of fruits and vegetables, purified or filtered water. *"And he shewed me a pure river of water of life, clear as crystal, proceeding out of the throne of God and of the Lamb. In the midst of the street of it, and on either side of the river, was there the tree of life, which bare twelve manner of fruits, and yielded her fruit every month, and the leaves of the tree were for the healing of the nations."* (Revelations 22: 1-2)

The conventional treatments like radiation and chemotherapy, though useful, have horrendous side effects like hair loss and vomiting. I read of a new natural treatment which involved the stimulation of my immune system so that tumors are destroyed by the NK cells. This treatment is derived from a substance found in certain Japanese mushrooms called Active Hexose Correlated Compound or AHCC in capsule form. It is supposed to increase the natural killer (NK) cells.

Is this a wonder "natural" drug? *"In the midst of the street of it, and on either side of the river, was there the tree of life, which bear twelve manner of fruits and yielded her fruit every month and the leaves of the tree were for the healing of the nation."* (Revelation 22: 2) It is supposed to provide extra power to help my body fight the cancer as its primary function is the strengthening of the immune system, it will also act as a deterrent against any disease. We have an immune system to protect us against bacteria, viruses and/or substances harmful to our *fearfully and wonderfully made* body.

Instead of looking for a reason and asking "why me", "what did I do wrong", "woe is me", why not look upon it as a blessed opportunity to be used as an instrument to be of service to others? To comfort others as we ourselves will be comforted by God our Father who is referred to as *"the Father of mercies and the God of all comfort who comforteth us in all our tribulation that we may be able to comfort them which are in any trouble by the comfort wherewith we ourselves are comforted of God."* (11 Cor. 1: 3-4)

We take so much for granted until something happens for us to take stock. We each have various stages of challenges. This could have been a *"dark night of the soul"*, but I chose not to make it so. It could have been a death sentence but, again, I chose not to make it so.

"The Dark Night of the Soul" was a classic piece of work written in the 16th century by Saint John of the Cross. His writing was about the personal spiritual journey. Since then, the deep trials we go through that almost break us so that we say *"My God, My God why have you forsaken me?"* have been termed *"the dark night of the soul."*

Your *dark night of the soul* should make you pay attention to everything that is taking place within it for the possibility exists that in it, there is something that can be shared with others to benefit them. Dark nights of the soul are never for us alone but for others, as well. *"Wherefore lift up the hands which hang down and the feeble knees and make straight paths for your feet."* In other words, stop your moaning and groaning, be active, do something. Take action!

I took action against the dis-ease by doing the research into it. When you take action, you feel powerful. Fear masks power. Get rid of the fear and the power emerges. Remember, we were not given *a spirit of fear but of power and a sound mind;* a sound mind to have the courage to take the necessary action. Once you decide to take action and step out, things happen.

We are afraid of what we do not understand. I decided to research this dis-ease of the body and in doing so I have knowledge which I would not have had otherwise. *"My people perish for lack of knowledge."* With knowledge comes wisdom. The wisdom gained from the knowledge has taught me that there is nothing to fear but fear itself.

Fear paralyzes and prevents us from taking action. Fear should propel us into taking action. Our beliefs influence our mind which influence our body. Our beliefs can limit us or expand us. Beliefs create emotions which create feelings. Our belief creates our reality. We have the power to create. If true, what we can create are healthy healing thoughts.

I avoided saying **"I have cancer"** because I did not own it as it is not something good that I wanted. I disarmed it by saying **"I was diagnosed with cancer."** It is not something for anyone to want to have. You may ask *"What is the difference in the phrasing, it's all the same."* Not to me. You see, I split myself into two parts – the physical and the spiritual. The spiritual part "I", the inner part, does not have cancer but the physical part, the outer part, was diagnosed with it. Take some fruits, for example. The skin is getting old and wrinkled but the inner part, the flesh is still good, it is not wrinkled. What do you do? You remove the skin and eat the good flesh.

The diagnosis of cancer is on the outside, therefore do what has to be done to restore it. Remember, this is my experience whether or not you agree or disagree. If cancer were a good thing, people would have rejoiced when they heard that someone had it instead of expressing horror. A friend e-mailed me that she shed a tear when she heard about my diagnosis. I know it was heartless of me but I laughed for there was nothing to cry about. She probably saw it as a death sentence.

The feel of your body will tell you when you have made a right decision; if you feel comfort, it is right, if discomfort, your decision is wrong. Radiation and/or chemotherapy must seem right to me for me to use it and since it does not, I decided not to take them. It should also be used in the choice of medication, treatment and diet for no two persons are the same. What may be good for the persons you read or hear about may not be good for you. Decide your own treatment and diet by the feelings in your body.

CHAPTER VI

Non-Conventional Treatments

Raw Food
Apparently, the way our bodies react to foreign invaders is the same way in which it reacts to cooked foods, hence the

recommendation for raw foods. They release more white blood cells.

Our food should be our medicine but between 30 to 85% of its nutrition is destroyed in cooking, so says one research. Fresh, raw foods have the highest levels of enzymes which promote life. Enzymes are needed by minerals and vitamins to reach the cells. Alas, our soil is deficient in minerals that are needed for our health, which makes our body suitable for bacteria, viruses and parasites.

Our body reacts to cooked food as if it were a foreign invader and releases more white blood cells. When eating raw foods with cooked foods, the immune response is neutral. Some experts say our raw foods should be 80-85% and cooked foods should be 15-20%. The body absorbs what it needs from raw foods. While raw foods build the immune system, some fruits and vegetables have nutrients that kill cancer cells and can also stop the spread of cancer. Some of these foods are carrots, broccoli, cabbage, Brussels sprouts, cauliflower, peppers, asparagus, pineapple, watermelon, purple grapes, apricots and seeds, blueberries, beetroot, beets, turmeric, apples, peaches, tomatoes.

Even so, unless we grow these ourselves or have access to where they are grown, some of the nutrients will be destroyed by the time they reach the markets or supermarkets. How many days travel before they reach us? Sure, they fill us up when eaten but how much nutrient do they contain?

The basis for the raw food diet is taken from Genesis 1:29 which says: *"And God said, Behold I have given you every herb bearing seed, which is upon the face of all the earth and every tree in the which is the fruit of a tree yielding seed to you it shall be for meat."*

Juicing is recommended for fruits or vegetables because it makes the nutrients not only more digestible but extracts more of the nutrients. More nutrients can be consumed in a shorter amount of time. I drank so much carrot juice that when I visited my doctor she was concerned by the yellowness of my palms until I told her what had caused it.

Exercise is important in the building of the immune system as well as the lymph and circulatory systems. It increases oxygen.

The importance of a good cancer diet is that it can help build the immune system and kill cancer cells. The immune system is the body's defense against diseases. It is made up of cells, tissues and organs which work to protect the body.

AHCC or Active Hexose Correlated Compound is a compound derived from a mushroom used for medicinal purposes in Japan for cancer and other diseases of immune deficiency. It not only regulates the activity of several types of white blood cells but increases the activity of natural killer cells. Natural killer cells identify abnormal cells and destroy them.

It can stimulate the immune system to fight T-cells which directly attack cells taken over by cancer; interleukin which helps the immune system to stimulate growth and activity of white blood cells, microphages which consumes foreign materials and protect the body from infection. Since the health food stores do not carry it here, a friend in Canada mailed me a bottle in tablet form.

Cancerbush known as Kankerbos by the southern Africans has been used for centuries to treat cancer. It has powerful immune boosting properties. My nephew sent me a bottle in tablet form from the UK.

Antioxidants inhibit oxidation and act as protectors for the body against the damages of free radicals. Free radicals are by-products of the chemical processes of the body which attack healthy cells, changing their DNA thus causing tumors to grow.

Selenium, an antioxidant, is a mineral found in small amounts in the body's tissues. As the body ages, selenium in the cells decreases, the immune system goes haywire and the body is susceptible to disease. If taken in large amounts it can be toxic. Some sources of selenium are grains, sunflower seeds, Brazilian nuts, onions, mushrooms, broccoli, seafood and garlic. It helps protects cells from harmful free radicals. Together selenium and Vitamin E are a team. Selenium protects within the cells and Vitamin E protects the outer cell membranes.

CoenzymeQ10 referred to as CoQ10 is an antioxidant used for the burning of oxygen within the cells which is necessary for them to do their job. It protects the body's tissues from wear and tear by destroying free radicals – unstable molecules which steal electrons at the cellular level. It also reacts with another enzyme so that cells can convert protein, fat and carbohydrates into energy.

Vitamin E, a fat-soluble vitamin (attaches to fat) found in vegetable oils, wheat germ, nuts, avocados, etc., is best taken with a meal containing some fat. There are two kinds: synthetic (dl-alpha-tocopherol) and natural (d-alpha-tocopherol). The natural kind is better absorbed and stays longer in the body than the synthetic kind. It can help in the protection of cells from damages that can lead to cancer.

Sesame Oil has a high antioxidant content. The seeds from which it is derived contain many health benefits, minerals, antioxidants and vitamins. In the tissues under the skin, the oil neutralizes oxygen radicals as it penetrates quickly into the skin, entering the blood stream and circulating. It regulates the cells, slowing down cell growth and replication.

On the skin, oil soluble toxins are attracted to sesame seed oil molecules which are washed away with hot water and soap. As the oil is absorbed through the skin, internally, the oil molecules attract oil soluble toxins and carry them away into the bloodstream and then out of the body as waste.

Green tea cuts off the blood supply to newly developing cancer cells.

Light Therapy stimulates the body's immune response: Apparently, a portion of your blood is removed and placed under ultraviolet light killing what is contagious in the blood cells. It is then injected back into your body. This stimulates the immune system and re-organizes your body's defenses *"because the darkness is past and the true light now shineth"* (1 John 2: 8)

The healing properties of ultraviolet light were first demonstrated by Niels Ryberg Finsen in the 1800's. It not only reduces the level of infection but strengthens the immune system. There are supposedly no side effects.

Sounds have vibrations. Words have sounds. Sounds can be healing. Jesus used sound for healing in the case of the centurion's servant whom he healed by just speaking the word.

(Matthew 8: 5-8) Words as sounds have power to heal. *He sent his word and healed them...* (Psalms 107: 20) Not only the words were used to heal but possibly the sound of the words, since sounds carry; they reverberate – echo and re-echo.

He sendeth out his word, and melteth them; he causeth his wind to blow and the waters flow... (Psalms 147: 18) The vibrational sound of the voice as the words were uttered, melted the ice, as well as causing the wind to blow and the waters to flow.

Sounds can heal as well as irritate. *"It is better to dwell in a corner of the housetop than with a brawling woman in a wide house." "It is better to dwell in the wilderness than with a contentious and an angry woman."* (Proverbs 21: 9, 19) It is not only her words but the sound of her voice that aggravates. It is a vexation to the spirit. It grates (makes a harsh, grinding sound) upon the body.

When a mother is singing to put her baby to sleep, it is not the words of the song but the sound of the mother's music. The world is made up of sounds – some pleasant and some not so pleasant. *"A continual dropping in a very rainy day and a contentious woman are alike."* (Proverbs 27: 15) In other words, the sound of the rain as it drops continually and the sound of the voice of a contentious woman are alike.

Sounds have the power to heal us, to soothe us or to have the opposite effect. When God withdrew His spirit from Saul and placed an evil spirit upon him that troubled him, his servants knew that only the sound of music could have made him well. *"And it came to pass, when the evil spirit from God was upon Saul, that David took an harp, and played with his hand;*

so Saul was refreshed and was well, and the evil spirit departed from him." (1 Samuel 16: 23)

As a child growing up, I remembered my mother using sound as a method of healing when our chickens were knocked out either from crossing the road and being hit by a car or from throwing something at them. She used to put a calabash (gourd) over them and pounded on it creating a sound. It appears that the vibration from the sound penetrated into their body and as this penetration took place, the chickens came to life again. Since sound was used to restore the chickens' lives, why can't I use sound also to restore my life too?

The vibrational frequency from musical sound should work on me for both the chicken and I have the same Maker. I checked my music supply and selected a sound CD called *Spirit Trance* which is part of a set called *Sound Health, Sound Wealth* by Dr. Luanne Oakes. It is a one-hour CD layered with subliminal messages which I played every morning. It is a series of sounds. In this three-part set, there is also a CD which deals with healing every part of the body. It utilizes specific sound frequencies to access the body's DNA healing codes.

The sound of dripping water can be annoying at times but, if you listen attentively, the sound has a beat. One of the sounds that I enjoy listening to and which makes me feel good is the sound of raindrops on the roof. It is calming, soothing and puts a big grin on my face.

Sunlight

The sun can be viewed as medicine as its light converts the cholesterol on our skin into Vitamin D which helps in bone making. Vitamin D stimulates the absorption of calcium in the intestinal tract. Sunlight apparently provides immunity to cancer as it regulates the body's immune system. The absorption of the ultraviolet rays gives strength and vitality to the body.

Simple things like a beautiful sunset, soft ocean breezes, young animals or children at play and a sunrise create wonderment within the body in the form of peace and drive away the cares of this life as the mind is captured by the spiritual and not the physical.

Laughter raises the amount of natural killer cells in the blood and one of blood's jobs is to destroy tumour cells.

Coconut Oil supposedly has anticancer properties. In days gone by, the only oil used was coconut. How many people were diagnosed with cancer then?

Salt

Some diets cut out salt completely while others recommend sea salt. Salt is a vital mineral needed by the body as it carries nutrients to and from cells, among other functions. Yet, salt helps to retain fluid and can cause breast pain.

There is so much information out there about food, that it can be confusing knowing what to do. Just when you think you have your perfect meal plan, something negative is being said about some of the foods.

Do whatever you can instead of just relying on conventional therapy. Know your individualized body and work with it. What is good for another may not be good for you and vice versa. Since you were individually made for God's pleasure, He has a special interest in you. Trust Him.

Printed in the United States
By Bookmasters